Sarah Brown's
VEGETARIAN
MICROWAVE
Cookbook

Sarah Brown's
VEGETARIAN MICROWAVE
Cookbook

DORLING KINDERSLEY ● LONDON

Editor   Carolyn Ryden
Consultant Editor   Felicity Jackson
Art Editor   Anita Ruddell

Art Director   Anne-Marie Bulat
Editorial Director   Alan Buckingham

Photography   Clive Streeter

First published in Great Britain in 1987 by
Dorling Kindersley Limited,
9 Henrietta Street,
London WC2E 8PS

Second impression 1987

British Library Cataloguing in Publication Data
Brown, Sarah
   Sarah Brown's vegetarian microwave cookbook
   1. Vegetarian cookery   2. Microwave cookery
   1. Title
   641.5′ 636   TX837

   ISBN 0-86318-199-6 *(hardback)*
   ISBN 0-86318-244-5 *(paperback)*

Printed and bound in Italy by L.E.G.O.

CONTENTS

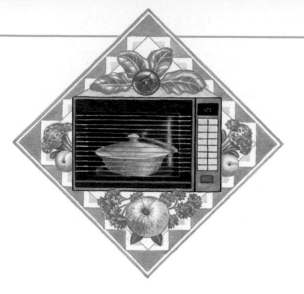

INTRODUCTION

As a recent convert to microwave cookery, I've found the past year of experimentation great fun and much more rewarding than I had anticipated. I had heard that vegetables could be wonderful cooked by microwave power but I was curious to find out how other foods cooked, particularly in terms of a vegetarian cuisine. My initial approach, however, was with a mixture of scepticism and trepidation. Cooking without any source of direct heat is a strange concept which seems to entail a whole new set of rules. Indeed, in its comparatively short life as a domestic item, a great mystique has developed about the microwave oven. I had a host of unanswered questions to solve: Was this revolutionary cooking appliance going to be a bonus or a bane? Did it cook from the inside out or the outside in? How could it be a time-saving device when there was so much to do every 15-seconds or so? I imagined I'd be spending my time dashing from one end of the kitchen to the other as those vital seconds that stood between success and an overcooked mess ticked by. I also wondered how it could be an asset in a vegetarian kitchen when it didn't seem to save any time cooking such basic ingredients as grains, pulses and pasta? And I had heard plenty of stories about anaemic cakes, soft pastry, pallid breads, collapsing soufflés and exploding eggs. People made it sound extremely daunting and even hazardous with an alarming number of scare stories circulating about leaking ovens, radiated food and other proclaimed dangers.

To put these conflicting ideas into perspective and satisfy my own curiosity, I set about investigating the microwave oven's potential. I soon learnt that it isn't quite like putting any other gadget into your kitchen. With something like a food processor for example, it's obvious what it will and will not do and it's relatively easy to understand how it operates. With items like freezers and conventional cookers, you need only a few trials to find out what works well in a new model. With a microwave oven, however, you not only have to get used to a new piece of equipment, but also to an entirely new method of cooking. There is absolutely nothing difficult about it, but it does take some time to adjust initially. Techniques such as stirring, arranging and covering foods are all far more crucial in the microwave than in conventional cookery.

It's important to understand their functions and to know when to apply them to use the microwave successfully. I've given clear explanations about these techniques on pages 124-128.

I soon began to understand how essential timing is in microwave cookery. Foods react differently to microwave energy according to their composition. With some dishes it is vital to watch the seconds pass, other dishes can be left to stand and finish cooking until you are ready. It all seemed fiddly at first, but I quickly discovered how many small tasks can be done in 30 seconds or one minute while waiting for the timing signal to sound.

Once I was familiar with the process and the techniques, I appreciated how different foods cook by microwave energy. There can be no doubt that a microwave oven is marvellous for cooking vegetables. It's easy and quick and preserves the maximum number of nutrients. The flavours are fresh, almost as concentrated as in raw vegetables, and the colours remain rich, while the texture can be firm yet tender. I either cook them lightly as if steamed on the hob, or I extend the time by a few minutes for a softer finish if I want to make a purée. When having a dinner party, I leave the vegetables until the very last minute to preserve their colour, texture, flavour and nutritional value And an extra bonus for anyone on their own is being able to cook small amounts of several varieties without having to use different pans.

Vegetarian cookery relies quite heavily on sauces and these are extremely simple to make in a microwave oven. I think it's marvellous to be able to infuse milk in a measuring jug and save on washing up, but also roux-based mixtures are less likely to form lumps and sauces in general are unlikely to stick or burn. You can even make small quantities in a suitable serving dish or sauce boat to take directly to the table.

The vegetarian staples of pulses and grains, and grain by-products such as pasta, are not particularly time-saving in a microwave as all need to be cooked in large volumes of water. However, you do gain in other ways. The containers are easier to clean and grains in particular remain separate and retain a good texture. Another distinct advantage is that grains, pasta and pulses all reheat extremely well in a microwave oven. I try to keep a supply of these ready-cooked so I can make an accompanying sauce or vegetable dish then reheat the grains, pasta or pulses to have a meal ready in minutes.

I was amazed at how quickly dishes of a more dense nature such as nut roasts, grain or bean savouries and steamed puddings could be cooked, saving enormous amounts of energy as well as time. It is important to have a well-flavoured mixture as the individual tastes don't have the same time to blend and develop as in conventional cookery. I find that some dishes do improve by being made in advance and then reheated so that the flavours have time to mellow and permeate a dish. I have indicated this in recipes but it is often a matter of individual taste.

The microwave oven should by no means be limited to main courses and vegetables. Fruit dishes cook wonderfully well, keeping their full flavour, texture and colour. Preserves can be made in small quantities without filling the kitchen with steam. Breads, cakes and biscuits are possible but they can be tricky and the results are not the same as in conventional baking. Using wholegrain products improves their colour and flavour as well as their nutritional content. I have suggested other ways of enhancing their appearance and texture in the recipes on page 102-112.

One of the greatest advantages of having a microwave is the way that it reheats food without it drying out, discolouring, or losing its flavour or nutritional content. Use it to reheat complete dishes or individual portions if you are coping with a family that eats at different times. It will help you make the most of your leftovers too.

For people like me, who frequently cook for one, a microwave oven is a real asset. It conserves energy by cooking food directly instead of heating up a whole oven cavity or a pan of water. The cooking times are so fast that you don't have to spend any length of time in the kitchen when making a solitary meal, and washing up is kept to a minimum as you can cook the food on the plate or dish you wish to serve it on.

A microwave is also a marvellous addition to any kitchen with a freezer as it takes much of the waiting out of defrosting. Most vegetarian foods freeze well, either when made up into complete dishes or as separate items such as cooked pulses, grains, sauces and vegetables. Speeding up the defrosting process means you can cope with meals in an emergency and feed unexpected guests at a moment's notice.

Part of the reason a microwave oven is so versatile is that it is virtually an oven and a hob in one and performs most of their functions in a fraction of the time. It can cope with those methods of cooking that involve some form of moisture — braising, boiling, baking, stewing and steaming — with the advantage that it is far quicker and cleaner than conventional methods. You cannot use a microwave for deep-fat frying, but this is a method that health-conscious cooks shouldn't be thinking of using very often! In fact, a microwave oven can positively encourage healthier eating habits. Whole meals become so easy to prepare that you should be able to avoid falling into the unhealthy syndrome of nibbles and snacks instead of complete meals.

Apart from the saving of time and energy when cooking by microwave, there are other benefits in terms of safety. Foods are much less likely to burn and there is little chance of you burning yourself. There are no hot surfaces and the controls are simple to operate, making them suitable for old people and children to use. Although microwave ovens have been the subject of some adverse criticism, the majority is quite unfounded and probably stems from fear and ignorance. If you are worried about what microwaves are, be reassured by the words of an American professor of physics who has stated that the risk of receiving harmful radiation from a microwave oven can be compared to ''getting a skin tan from the moon'', and turn to page 114. All microwave ovens must fulfil extremely high safety standards and are rigorously checked before leaving the manufacturer.

I hope you'll enjoy the ideas I've developed especially for this book, but don't forget many of your old favourite recipes will probably convert for the microwave. I've supplied some advice on how to try this on page 130. I certainly don't see the microwave oven replacing a conventional cooker but the two can be used to complement one another. I'm sure that you'll still prefer to cook some dishes conventionally; I know that I prefer bread and pastry baked by traditional methods. However, my microwave oven is in use every day and has become an indispensable part of my kitchen, far from being the dust-collecting gadget I thought it might turn out to be.

Sarah Brown

COOKING TIMES
AND TECHNIQUES

Basic cooking times and techniques are provided on the following pages for a wide range of vegetarian ingredients using 500W, 600W and 700W ovens. The need to underestimate rather than overestimate cooking and reheating times cannot be stressed strongly enough. Do not be afraid to open the oven door to examine how foods are progressing. Test frequently for readiness and stir, turn or rearrange as instructed.

Always test after the shortest time given, although timings will vary according to quantity and the age and size of individual ingredients. As a general rule, when doubling the amount of food cook for between a third and half the time again.

Timings here are provided for fresh, frozen and dried products. To reheat canned foods, simply transfer the contents to a suitable dish and FULL for 2-4 mins. 600W (*1-3 mins. 700W; 3-5 mins. 500W*), stirring once or twice.

Fresh Brussels sprouts

Brassicas and leaves

This group of vegetables frequently suffers from overcooking and can be limp, tasteless and unappreciated as a result. To enjoy their fresh flavour and crisp texture, cook them in the microwave for the minimum amount of time with the minimum amount of water. Simply cook for a little longer if you prefer a softer consistency.

Frozen Brussels sprouts

Fresh broccoli

Frozen broccoli

BRUSSELS SPROUTS

Fresh

Quantity	Cooking time on FULL (in mins)		
	500W	600W	700W
225g (8oz)	5-6	**4-5**	3-4
450g (1lb)	8-10	**7-8**	6-7

Cooking technique Wash and trim. Cut a cross in each base then place in a dish. Add 30ml (2 tbsp) water. Cover and cook, stirring once or twice. Allow to stand for 2-3 mins.

Frozen

Quantity	Cooking time on FULL (in mins)		
	500W	600W	700W
225g (8oz)	8-9	**6-7**	5-6

Cooking technique Place in a dish and cover. Stir 2 or 3 times. Allow to stand for 3-5 mins.

CAULIFLOWER

Fresh

Quantity	Cooking time on FULL (in mins)		
	500W	600W	700W
225g (8oz)	6-8	**4-6**	3-5
450g (1lb)	10-12	**8-10**	6-8

Cooking technique Wash and break into small, even-sized florets. Place in a dish with 30-45ml (2-3 tbsp) water. Stir during cooking. Stand for 2-3 mins. To cook whole, trim off the outer leaves and stem. Cut a cross in the base. Place in a bag, secure loosely and put on a plate, base up. Turn over halfway through and half turn the plate every 30 secs. Stand for at least 3 mins.

Frozen

Quantity	Cooking time on FULL (in mins)		
	500W	600W	700W
225g (8oz)	6-10	**5-8**	4-6

Cooking technique Cook covered but stir or shake twice. Allow to stand for 3-5 mins.

Fresh cauliflower

BROCCOLI

Fresh

Quantity	Cooking time on FULL (in mins)		
	500W	600W	700W
225g (8oz)	5-6	**4-5**	3-4
450g (1lb)	6-10	**5-8**	4-7

Cooking technique Wash, remove any tough stalks and cut a slit in any mature stalks. Arrange in a dish with the heads toward the centre. Add 30ml (2 tbsp) water and cover. Rearrange halfway through the cooking time. Allow to stand for 2-3 mins.

Frozen

Quantity	Cooking time on FULL (in mins)		
	500W	600W	700W
225g (8oz)	8-11	**6-9**	5-8

Cooking technique Leave in the bag, pierced, or place in a dish and cover. Stir or shake once or twice during the cooking time. Allow to stand for 3-5 mins.

Frozen cauliflower

Fresh Savoy cabbage

Fresh red cabbage

Fresh Chinese leaves

Fresh spinach

Frozen spinach

CHINESE LEAVES

Fresh

Quantity	Cooking time on FULL (in mins)		
	500W	**600W**	700W
225g (8oz)	3-5	**2-4**	2-4
450g (1lb)	8-10	**6-8**	5-7

Cooking technique Wash and remove damaged leaves. Trim the stalk and shred the leaves. Place in a dish and add 30ml (2 tbsp) water. Cook covered, stirring once or twice during the time. Allow to stand for 2-3 mins.

SPINACH

Fresh

Quantity	Cooking time on FULL (in mins)		
	500W	**600W**	700W
225g (8oz)	2-5	**2-4**	2-3
450g (1lb)	4-8	**3-6**	2-5

Cooking technique Wash and rinse well, discarding any damaged leaves. Cook covered without adding any water. Stir halfway through. Allow to stand for 2-3 mins.

Frozen

Quantity	Cooking time on FULL (in mins)		
	500W	**600W**	700W
225g (8oz)	6-9	**5-7**	4-6
450g (1lb)	9-11	**7-9**	6-8

Cooking technique Place in a dish and cover. Do not add water. Stir once during cooking.

CABBAGE (All varieties)

Fresh

Quantity	Cooking time on FULL (in mins)		
	500W	**600W**	700W
225g (8oz)	3-5	**2-4**	2-4
450g (1lb)	8-10	**6-8**	5-7

Cooking technique Discard any damaged leaves. Wash and shred. Place in a dish with 2 tbsp water. Omit the water when cooking young, green cabbage and reduce to 15ml (1 tbsp) when cooking Chinese cabbage. Stir once during cooking. Allow to stand for 2-4 mins. Alternatively, cook in a little sunflower margarine in a covered dish. Stir once during cooking and stand for 2 mins. When stewing red cabbage, extend the cooking time by about 2 mins. (see p.69).

Fresh white cabbage

Shoots and bulbs

Asparagus

Always choose firm, crisp vegetables and avoid those that are yellowing, wilted or damaged. Most shoots and bulbs require a little liquid or fat to tenderize in the oven so follow the guidelines below, testing after the shortest time given. Stir or rearrange the vegetables halfway through to ensure even cooking.

Chicory

Celery

ASPARAGUS
Fresh

Quantity	Cooking time on FULL (in mins)		
	500W	**600W**	700W
225g (8oz)	6-10	**5-8**	4-6
450g (1lb)	8-12	**7-10**	6-8

Cooking technique Trim off woody stems and arrange on a dish with the tender tips pointing in to the centre. Sprinkle with 15ml (1 tbsp) water. Cover and cook. Rearrange the spears, keeping the tips to the centre of the dish, halfway through the cooking time. Thicker ends should be tender when pierced with a knife. Allow to stand for 3 mins.

Frozen

Quantity	Cooking time on FULL (in mins)		
	500W	**600W**	700W
275g (10oz)	8-11	**6-9**	5-8

Cooking technique Place in a dish and cover. Separate and rearrange during the cooking time, keeping the tips in the centre. Allow to stand for 5 mins.

CHICORY
Fresh

Quantity	Cooking time on FULL (in mins)		
	500W	**600W**	700W
4 heads	7-10	**6-8**	5-7

Cooking technique Trim the heads, discarding any damaged leaves. Slice in two lengthways and arrange in a casserole dish, narrower parts to the centre. Add 15ml (1 tbsp) lemon juice and 15ml (1 tbsp) water. Cover and cook. Rearrange halfway through the cooking time, moving heads from the edge to the centre of the dish. Allow to stand for 3 mins.

KOHLRABI
Fresh

Quantity	Cooking time on FULL (in mins)		
	500W	**600W**	700W
450g (1lb)	10-12	**8-10**	6-8

Cooking technique Peel and chop into even-sized pieces. Add 60ml (4 tbsp) water and cook covered. Stir once during the cooking time. Stand for 3 mins.

Sliced celery

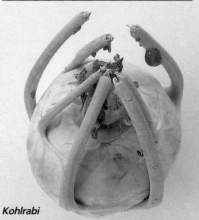

Kohlrabi

CELERY
Fresh

Quantity	Cooking time on FULL (in mins)		
	500W	**600W**	700W
225g (8oz)	6-8	**5-7**	4-6
450g (1lb)	10-12	**8-10**	6-8

Cooking technique Separate the stems. Wash, trim and cut into 1cm ($\frac{1}{2}$ in) slices. Add 60ml (4 tbsp) water and cover. Stir halfway through the cooking time. Allow to stand for 3 mins.

Onions

Frozen
onion slices

Leek

Fennel

ONIONS
Fresh

Quantity	Cooking time on FULL (in mins)		
	500W	**600W**	700W
225g (8oz)	4-6	**3-5**	2-4

Cooking technique Peel and slice. Add 30ml (2 tbsp) water or cook in 15ml (1 tbsp) of oil, preheated for 1 min. Cover and stir during cooking. Extend the cooking time by a few minutes when cooking larger quantities or if you want them stewed until soft. To bake them whole with a stuffing, cook uncovered for double the time. Leave to stand for 3 mins.

Frozen

Quantity	Cooking time on FULL (in mins)		
	500W	**600W**	700W
225g (8oz)	5-7	**4-6**	3-5

Cooking technique Pierce the pack or place in a dish and cover. Shake or stir once. Leave to stand for 3 mins.

GLOBE ARTICHOKE
Fresh

Quantity	Cooking time on FULL (in mins)		
	500W	**600W**	700W
1 head	6-7	**5-6**	4-5
2 heads	9-10	**7-8**	6-7

Cooking technique Wash, cut off stalk and lower leaves. Snip the leaf tips. Place in a large roasting bag or covered dish with 60ml (4 tbsp) water and 30ml (2 tbsp) lemon juice. Rotate or rearrange once during the cooking time. Test if ready by removing one of the leaves—it should come away easily. Drain and stand for 3-5 mins. before serving with butter.

Sliced leek

FENNEL
Fresh

Quantity	Cooking time on FULL (in mins)		
	500W	**600W**	700W
225g (8oz)	5-7	**4-6**	3-5
450g (1lb)	7-10	**6-8**	5-6

Cooking technique Trim and wash the outside leaves. Slice in half lengthways. Place in a dish or bag with 30ml (2 tbsp) water. Cover and cook, stirring or rearranging twice. Leave to stand for 3 mins. This method results in a crisp vegetable. Cook for 1 or 2 mins. longer if you prefer a softer texture.

LEEKS
Fresh

Quantity	Cooking time on FULL (in mins)		
	500W	**600W**	700W
225g (8oz)	3-6	**3-5**	2-4
450g (1lb)	6-8	**5-7**	4-6

Cooking technique Wash, trim and slice evenly. Add 30ml (2 tbsp) water, cover and cook. Stir once during cooking. Allow to stand for 3-5 mins. before serving.

Globe artichoke

Fruit vegetables

Fruit vegetables contain light, moist flesh which cooks quickly in its own juices in the microwave. Those with thin skins can be baked whole but remember always to pierce the skin first so that steam can escape without causing a messy explosion in the oven. The watery flesh of marrows and aubergines takes on flavours particularly well. For a tasty side dish, simply slice them and cook covered adding a mixture of herbs and spices. For a more substantial meal, try the recipes on pages 54, 64 and 66.

Plum tomatoes

Aubergine

TOMATOES
Fresh

Quantity	Cooking time on FULL (in mins)		
	500W	**600W**	700W
225g (8oz)	3-6	**3-5**	2-4
450g (1lb)	6-8	**5-7**	4-6

Cooking technique Cut in half or into slices. Flavour with black pepper and basil, marjoram, thyme or oregano. Cover and stir once during cooking. The large beef tomatoes make excellent containers. Follow the recipe on p.49 and fill with any cooked whole grain, chopped nut or vegetable mixture.

Beef tomato

Red pepper

PEPPERS
Fresh

Quantity	Cooking time on FULL (in mins)		
	500W	**600W**	700W
225g (8oz)	2-3	**2-3**	1-2
450g (1lb)	5-7	**4-6**	3-5

Cooking technique Remove the central stalk and seeds. Cut into rings, slices or halves. Cook, covered, in 15ml (1 tbsp) water or hot oil. Stir or rearrange once during cooking.

Sliced aubergine

AUBERGINE
Fresh

Quantity	Cooking time on FULL (in mins)		
	500W	**600W**	700W
225g (8oz)	3-6	**3-5**	2-4
450g (1lb)	6-10	**5-8**	4-6

Cooking technique To bake whole, trim, then pierce the skin. Wrap in absorbent paper. Turn over and rearrange once during cooking. Allow to stand for 4 mins. Serve whole, sliced or mashed with lemon juice. For stuffed aubergines, cook for the minimum time and stand. Scoop out the flesh and mix with a cooked grain and vegetable filling before replacing in the shell. Reheat for 2-4 mins. before serving. To stew sliced aubergines, cover and cook in 15ml (1 tbsp) heated oil or water, following the timings above. Stir once during cooking. Season with salt, pepper and fresh herbs. Allow to stand for 4 mins.

Green pepper

Yellow pepper

Courgettes

Frozen courgette slices

Marrow

Pumpkin

COURGETTES
Fresh

Quantity	Cooking time on FULL (in mins)		
	500W	**600W**	700W
225g (8oz)	5-7	**4-6**	3-5
450g (1lb)	7-10	**6-8**	5-7

Cooking technique Cut into strips or rings. Dot with sunflower margarine or allow to stew in own juices. Add herbs and ground black pepper for extra flavour. Cover and stir once during cooking. Simply cut the ends off baby courgettes and cook them whole. Allow to stand for 3 mins.

Frozen

Quantity	Cooking time on FULL (in mins)		
	500W	**600W**	700W
225g (8oz)	8-11	**7-9**	6-7
450g (1lb)	11-14	**9-11**	7-9

Cooking technique Pierce the bag. Shake during cooking. Allow to stand for 3 mins.

PUMPKIN
Fresh

Quantity	Cooking time on FULL (in mins)		
	500W	**600W**	700W
450g (1lb)	7-10	**6-8**	5-6

Cooking technique Halve and remove stem and base so each half can sit on a plate. Cover with greaseproof paper and cook one half at a time. Test for tenderness as timing will depend on age and size. Allow to stand for 2 mins. before scooping out the seeds and pith. Purée the flesh with added coriander and garlic.

MARROW
Fresh

Quantity	Cooking time on FULL (in mins)		
	500W	**600W**	700W
225g (8oz)	5-7	**4-6**	3-5
450g (1lb)	7-10	**6-8**	5-7

Cooking technique Peel if the skin is tough. Slice in half and remove the seeds and fibrous flesh. Cut into cubes. Add herbs and ground black pepper to enhance the flavour. Cover and allow to stew in own juices. Stir once during cooking. Stand for 3 mins.

Pods and seeds

You need to add very little water to fresh peas and beans and none at all to frozen. Do not add salt before cooking, however, since it can dehydrate the vegetables. For evenly cooked results, use a shallow dish and spread out the vegetables rather than heaping them up. These timings produce peas and beans that are still crunchy to eat. If you prefer a softer texture, cook for 1 or 2 minutes longer but do avoid overcooking.

Fresh peas

Frozen peas

GARDEN PEAS

Fresh

Quantity	Cooking time on FULL (in mins)		
	500W	600W	700W
225g (8oz)	6-8	**5-7**	4-6
450g (1lb)	10-12	**8-10**	7-8

Cooking technique Shell. Add 30ml (2 tbsp) water. Cover and stir during cooking. Allow to stand for 3-5 mins.

Frozen

Quantity	Cooking time on FULL (in mins)		
	500W	600W	700W
225g (8oz)	5-6	**4-5**	3-4
450g (1lb)	9-10	**7-8**	6-7

Cooking technique Add a knob of butter and cover. Stir during cooking. Allow to stand for 2-3 mins.

Frozen petit pois

PETIT POIS

Frozen

Quantity	Cooking time on FULL (in mins)		
	500W	600W	700W
225g (8oz)	4-6	**3-5**	2-4
450g (1lb)	7-10	**6-8**	5-7

Cooking technique Add a knob of butter and cover. Stir once during cooking. Allow to stand for 2 mins.

Fresh mangetout

RUNNER BEANS

Fresh

Quantity	Cooking time on FULL (in mins)		
	500W	600W	700W
225g (8oz)	6-8	**5-7**	4-6
450g (1lb)	8-11	**7-9**	6-8

Cooking technique String and slice. Add 30ml (2 tbsp) water and cover. Stir 2-3 times during cooking. Leave to stand for 2 mins. Allow longer for larger beans.

Fresh runner beans

MANGETOUT

Fresh

Quantity	Cooking time on FULL (in mins)		
	500W	600W	700W
225g (8oz)	7-9	**6-7**	5-6
450g (1lb)	10-11	**8-9**	6-7

Cooking technique Wash and trim. Add 30ml (2 tbsp) water and cover. Stir during cooking. Allow to stand for 2-3 mins.

Fresh bobby beans

BOBBY BEANS

Fresh

Quantity	Cooking time on FULL (in mins)		
	500W	600W	700W
225g (8oz)	5-6	**4-5**	3-4
450g (1lb)	6-9	**5-7**	4-6

Cooking technique Wash and trim. Add 30ml (2 tbsp) water and cover. Stir during cooking. Allow to stand for 2-3 mins.

Fresh French beans

FRENCH BEANS

Fresh

Quantity	Cooking time on FULL (in mins)		
	500W	600W	700W
225g (8oz)	6-9	**5-7**	4-6
450g (1lb)	9-11	**7-9**	6-8

Cooking technique Wash and trim. Add 45ml (3 tbsp) water and cover. Stir once during cooking. Allow to stand for 3 mins.

Frozen green beans

GREEN BEANS
Frozen

Quantity	Cooking time on FULL (in mins)		
	500W	600W	700W
225g (8oz)	8-10	**7-8**	6-7
450g (1lb)	10-12	**9-10**	8-9

Cooking technique Add a knob of butter. Cover. Stir once during cooking. Allow to stand for 5 mins.

Fresh broad beans

Frozen broad beans

BROAD BEANS
Fresh

Quantity	Cooking time on FULL (in mins)		
	500W	600W	700W
225g (8oz)	8-10	**6-8**	5-7
450g (1lb)	11-12	**9-10**	8-9

Cooking technique Shell. Add 45ml (3 tbsp) water and cover. Stir after 3 mins. and test after 5 mins. Dot with butter and allow to stand for 5 mins.

Frozen

Quantity	Cooking time on FULL (in mins)		
	500W	600W	700W
225g (8oz)	9-10	**7-8**	6-7
450g (1lb)	12-15	**10-12**	8-10

Cooking technique Add a knob of butter and cover. Stir once or twice during cooking. Allow to stand for 5 mins.

SWEETCORN
Frozen

Quantity	Cooking time on FULL (in mins)		
	500W	600W	700W
225g (8oz)	5-8	**4-6**	3-5
450g (1lb)	9-10	**7-8**	6-7

Cooking technique Add 30ml (2 tbsp) water or a knob of butter. Cover and stir during cooking. Allow to stand for 3 mins.

Fresh okra

OKRA
Fresh

Quantity	Cooking time on FULL (in mins)		
	500W	600W	700W
225g (8oz)	8-9	**6-7**	5-6
450g (1lb)	10-11	**8-9**	7-8

Cooking technique Trim and wash. Cook whole or cut into 2.5cm (1 in) lengths. Add 60ml (4 tbsp) water or 15ml (1 tbsp) preheated oil. Cover. Turn the bowl halfway through the cooking time. Stand for 3 mins.

Frozen corn-on-the-cob

Frozen sweetcorn

CORN-ON-THE-COB
Fresh

Quantity	Cooking time on FULL (in mins)		
	500W	600W	700W
1 225g (8oz)	5-6	**4-5**	3-4
2 450g (1lb)	8-10	**6-8**	5-7
4 900g (2lb)	10-12	**8-10**	7-9

Cooking technique Trim and wash. Add 15ml (1 tbsp) water per cob and cover. Turn over during cooking. Leave to stand 2-3 mins. Serve with butter. Alternatively, wrap individually in greased, greaseproof paper. Turn over and rearrange halfway through the cooking time. For baby cobs, cook by weight and reduce the time by 2 mins.

Frozen

Quantity	Cooking time on FULL (in mins)		
	500W	600W	700W
1 cob	4-5	**3-4**	2-3
2 cobs	8-9	**6-7**	5-6

Cooking technique Dot with butter and wrap in greaseproof paper. Turn over and rearrange halfway through cooking. Leave to stand for 3-5 mins.

Fresh corn-on-the-cob

Fresh baby corn-on-the-cob

Roots and tubers

All root vegetables cook well in the microwave, retaining their full flavour and texture. For the best results, cook potatoes, young beetroots, baby carrots and small turnips whole and then cut into slices before serving or adding to recipes. Follow the guidelines below and test for tenderness after the shortest times as these are always dependent upon age, size and quantity. Extend the timing if you want to purée the vegetables.

Fresh sweet potatoes

SWEET POTATOES

Fresh

Quantity	Cooking time on FULL (in mins)		
	500W	**600W**	700W
450g (1lb)	8-10	**6-8**	5-7

Cooking technique Select small, even-shaped potatoes. Scrub and remove any long tail parts. Pierce all over and space evenly around the edge of a plate. Cover and cook, turning over and rearranging halfway through the cooking time. Allow to stand for 2-3 mins. then dot with butter and fresh chopped parsley or mint. Serve whole or sliced.

POTATOES

Fresh

Quantity	Cooking time on FULL (in mins)		
	500W	**600W**	700W
225g (8oz)	5-6	**4-5**	3-4
450g (1lb)	10-15	**8-10**	6-8

Cooking technique Choose even-sized potatoes and scrub any soil off the skins. Pierce well all over and wrap in absorbent paper. Arrange in an evenly spaced circle on a plate and cook. Turn over and rearrange halfway through the cooking time. Allow to stand for 5 mins. Serve whole or sliced thinly as required. See p.82 for more suggestions.

BEETROOTS

Fresh

Quantity	Cooking time on FULL (in mins)		
	500W	**600W**	700W
450g (1lb)	12-15	**10-12**	8-10

Cooking technique Scrub small ones and remove their stems and bases. Pierce well on all sides then cook in a bag. Turn over and rearrange halfway through the cooking time. Allow to stand for 3-5 mins. then scrape off their skins. Serve whole or diced. If cooking large beetroots, peel and cut into thick, even-sized chunks. Cook covered for about half the length of time. Delicious served as a hot vegetable or chilled in salads.

Fresh, raw beetroot

Fresh parsnips

PARSNIPS

Fresh

Quantity	Cooking time on FULL (in mins)		
	500W	**600W**	700W
450g (1lb)	6-10	**5-8**	4-7

Cooking technique Peel, cut in half or slice into even-sized chunks or julienne strips and place in a dish. If cooking halves, arrange with the thinner ends toward the centre. Add 30ml (2 tbsp) water and some lemon juice. Cook covered and stir or rearrange halfway through. Allow to stand for 2-3 mins. then drain. Toss in butter and season.

TURNIPS

Fresh

Quantity	Cooking time on FULL (in mins)		
	500W	**600W**	700W
450g (1lb)	10-12	**8-10**	6-8

Cooking technique Peel and slice evenly, but leave baby turnips whole. Add 30ml (2 tbsp) water and cook covered until tender, stirring twice. Leave to stand for 3-5 mins. Drain well.

Fresh turnips

Fresh potatoes

Fresh baby carrots

Fresh carrot rings

Fresh carrot julienne strips

Frozen carrots

Frozen swede

Fresh swede

Fresh celeriac

CELERIAC

Fresh

Quantity	Cooking time on FULL (in mins)		
	500W	**600W**	700W
450g (1lb)	8-10	**6-8**	4-6

Cooking technique Scrub, trim and peel. Cut into julienne strips and place in a dish with 45ml (3 tbsp) water. Cover and cook, stirring once or twice during cooking. Drain well and toss in lemon juice. To blanch celeriac for salads, cook for half the length of time, stirring every minute. Then drain and toss in lemon juice. Serve with a dressing.

SWEDE

Fresh

Quantity	Cooking time on FULL (in mins)		
	500W	**600W**	700W
450g (1lb)	10-12	**8-10**	7-9

Cooking technique Peel and dice. Place in a dish with 30ml (2 tbsp) water. Cover and cook until tender, stirring once or twice. Drain well. Serve sprinkled with black pepper and chopped parsley. Swede is also delicious mashed with a little butter or margarine, yogurt and ground black pepper.

Frozen

Quantity	Cooking time on FULL (in mins)		
	500W	**600W**	700W
225g (8oz)	12-15	**10-12**	8-10

Cooking technique Place in a dish and add 60ml (4 tbsp) water. Cover and cook, stirring halfway through the time. Stand for 2 mins. then drain. See serving ideas above.

CARROTS

Fresh

Quantity	Cooking time on FULL (in mins)		
	500W	**600W**	700W
225g (8oz)	5-8	**4-6**	3-5
450g (1lb)	8-10	**6-8**	5-7

Cooking technique Wash and prepare as usual. Leave baby carrots whole but slice larger ones into julienne strips or rings. Place in a dish and add 30ml (2-3 tbsp) water. Cover and cook, stirring once or twice. Allow to stand for 2-3 mins.

Frozen

Quantity	Cooking time on FULL (in mins)		
	500W	**600W**	700W
225g (8oz)	6-8	**5-7**	4-6

Cooking technique Pierce the bag or pour the carrots into a dish and cover. Cook, stirring once or twice during the time. Allow to stand for 2-3 mins.

Frozen apple slices

Fruit

Frozen blackberries

All fruits can be cooked to produce excellent results in a microwave. Colour, flavour and texture are retained in full in the short cooking time, or you can stew fruits to make a soft purée by cooking for a few minutes longer. When testing the firmness of cooked fruits, allow for the fact that they will continue to soften after they have been removed from the oven.

Fresh blackberries

Fresh apple

APPLES

Fresh

Quantity	Cooking time on FULL (in mins)		
	500W	600W	700W
225g (8oz)	3-5	**3-4**	2-3
450g (1lb)	7-10	**6-8**	5-7

Cooking technique Peel, core and slice. Sprinkle with lemon juice and a little honey if you like them sweetened. Cover and stir once during cooking. Allow to stand for 3 mins. To bake whole apples, use the same cooking times, but remember that they will vary according to the size of the apples. Core and fill with a mixture of dried fruit, chopped nuts and a little margarine. Score round the centre to prevent bursting. Arrange in a circle and rearrange halfway through the cooking time. Allow to stand for 2 mins. Cook for a further 2 mins. if required.

Frozen

Quantity	Cooking time on FULL (in mins)		
	500W	600W	700W
225g (8oz)	2-5	**2-4**	2-3
450g (1lb)	6-10	**4-8**	5-7

Cooking technique Add a knob of butter and cover. Stir or shake during cooking. Leave to stand for 5 mins.

Fresh blueberries

Frozen blueberries

BLUEBERRIES AND BLACKCURRANTS

Fresh

Quantity	Cooking time on FULL (in mins)		
	500W	600W	700W
225g (8oz)	2-5	**2-4**	2-3
450g (1lb)	3-6	**3-5**	2-4

Cooking technique Top and tail, then wash the fruit. Add 15ml (1 tbsp) honey to make less sharp in flavour if preferred. Cover and stir once. Allow to stand for 3 mins.

Frozen

Quantity	Cooking time on FULL (in mins)		
	500W	600W	700W
225g (8oz)	3-6	**3-5**	2-4
450g (1lb)	4-7	**4-6**	3-5

Cooking technique Pierce freezer bag or place frozen fruit in a covered container. Stir once during cooking. Stand for 5 mins.

Frozen blackcurrants

Fresh blackcurrants

PLUMS

Fresh

Quantity	Cooking time on FULL (in mins)		
	500W	600W	700W
225g (8oz)	3-6	**3-5**	2-4
450g (1lb)	5-7	**4-6**	3-5

Cooking technique Wash, then slice each fruit in half and remove stones. Add a touch of cinnamon and grated lemon rind for extra flavour, or cook in 15-30ml (1-2 tbsp) red wine. Cover and stir once during cooking. Allow to stand for 5 mins.

BLACKBERRIES

Fresh

Quantity	Cooking time on FULL (in mins)		
	500W	600W	700W
225g (8oz)	2-5	**2-4**	2-3
450g (1lb)	3-6	**2-5**	2-4

Cooking technique Hull and wash. Cover. Stir once. Allow to stand for 3 mins.

Frozen

Quantity	Cooking time on FULL (in mins)		
	500W	600W	700W
225g (8oz)	3-6	**3-5**	2-4
450g (1lb)	4-7	**4-6**	3-5

Cooking technique Cover. Stir or shake once. Allow to stand for 5 mins.

Frozen redcurrants

Fresh redcurrants

REDCURRANTS

Fresh

Quantity	Cooking time on FULL (in mins)		
	500W	600W	700W
225g (8oz)	2-5	**2-4**	2-3
450g (1lb)	3-6	**2-5**	2-3

Cooking technique Top and tail, then wash. Cover and stir once during the cooking time. Redcurrants add colour to poached fruit, try them with pears or peaches, in mixed fruit compotes or crumbles.

Frozen

Quantity	Cooking time on FULL (in mins)		
	500W	600W	700W
225g (8oz)	3-6	**3-5**	2-4
450g (1lb)	4-7	**4-6**	3-5

Cooking technique Cover and stir or shake once during cooking. Stand for 5 mins.

Fresh cooking apple

Fresh plums

Fresh peach

PEACHES
Fresh

Quantity	Cooking time on FULL (in mins)		
	500W	**600W**	700W
225g (8oz)	3-6	**3-5**	2-4
450g (1lb)	5-7	**4-6**	3-5

Cooking technique Wash, cut in half and remove stones. Slice, quarter or leave as halves. Add 30ml (2 tbsp) water or fruit juice. Cover. Stir or rearrange once during cooking. Allow to stand for 3 mins.

Fresh nectarines

NECTARINES
Fresh

Quantity	Cooking time on FULL (in mins)		
	500W	**600W**	700W
225g (8oz)	3-6	**3-5**	2-4
450g (1lb)	5-7	**4-6**	3-5

Cooking technique Wash, cut in half and remove stones. Slice, quarter or leave as halves. Add 30ml (2 tbsp) water or fruit juice. Cover. Stir or rearrange once during cooking. Allow to stand for 3 mins.

Fresh greengages

GREENGAGES
Fresh

Quantity	Cooking time on FULL (in mins)		
	500W	**600W**	700W
225g (8oz)	3-6	**3-5**	2-4
450g (1lb)	5-7	**4-6**	3-5

Cooking technique Wash, cut in half and remove stones. Add 15ml (1 tbsp) water, or orange juice for a different flavour. Cover and cook, stirring once during the cooking time. Allow to stand for 3 mins.

BANANAS
Fresh

Quantity	Cooking time on FULL (in mins)		
	500W	**600W**	700W
2	2-3	**2-3**	1-2
4	3-5	**3-4**	2-3

Cooking technique Use firm bananas. Peel and place in a dish. Mix together the juice of 1 lemon and 15-30ml (1-2 tbsp) honey. Pour over the bananas. Cook uncovered and leave to stand for 2 mins. Serve with yogurt or flambé with rum. Heating alcohol in the microwave can be dangerous as it may ignite, so flambé in the conventional way.

Banana

Fresh apricots

APRICOTS
Fresh

Quantity	Cooking time on FULL (in mins)		
	500W	**600W**	700W
225g (8oz)	5-7	**4-6**	3-5
450g (1lb)	7-10	**6-8**	5-7

Cooking technique Wash, halve and remove stones. Leave halved or cut into slices. Add 15ml (1 tbsp) apple juice and some grated lemon peel if wished. Cover and stir once. Allow to stand for 3 mins.

Fresh pears

PEARS
Fresh

Quantity	Cooking time on FULL (in mins)		
	500W	**600W**	700W
225g (8oz)	3-5	**3-4**	2-3
450g (1lb)	6 8	**5-7**	4-6

Cooking technique Peel, then cut in half lengthways and remove the core. Arrange in a circular dish with the broadest ends at the outer edge. Pour over 30ml (2 tbsp) apple or orange juice and sprinkle in a little ginger. Cover and cook until tender. rearranging halfway through the time. Allow to stand for 3 mins.

RHUBARB
Fresh

Quantity	Cooking time on FULL (in mins)		
	500W	**600W**	700W
225g (8oz)	5-7	**4-6**	3-5
450g (1lb)	7-11	**6-9**	5-8

Cooking technique Trim, wash and cut into even 2.5cm (1 in) lengths. Place in a dish and sprinkle with grated orange peel or a little ground ginger. Cover. Stir twice during cooking. Allow to stand for 3 mins.

Fresh rhubarb

Dried fruit

Dried apricots

Hunza apricot

All dried fruit plump up and soften quickly in the microwave, eliminating the need for advance planning and hours of presoaking when using them as ingredients. Follow the guidelines for timings and liquid volume given below. The cooking times are almost the same for all microwave ovens because dried fruits reconstitute in water rather than by the action of microwaves. The longer you allow the fruit to stand, however, the softer and richer in flavour it becomes. For extra zest, cook in fruit juice or add some whole spices to the cooking liquid; try a stick of cinnamon, one or two cloves, or some allspice berries. Cook in a covered shallow dish to avoid evaporation.

Dried figs

DRIED APRICOTS

Quantity	Cooking time on FULL (in mins)		
	500W	**600W**	700W
100g (4oz)	6-10	**5-8**	5-8

Cooking technique Place in a bowl and cover with 600ml (1 pint) boiling water. Cover and cook, stirring once during cooking. Allow to stand for 10-30 mins.

HUNZA APRICOTS

Quantity	Cooking time on FULL (in mins)		
	500W	**600W**	700W
225g (8oz)	6-10	**5-8**	5-8

Cooking technique Place in a dish and cover with 900ml (1½ pints) of boiling water. Cover and cook, stirring once during cooking. Allow to stand for 10-30 mins.

Sultanas

Raisins

Currants

SULTANAS, RAISINS AND CURRANTS

Quantity	Cooking time on FULL (in mins)		
	500W	**600W**	700W
100g (4oz)	2-5	**2-4**	2-4

Cooking technique Place in a dish with 150ml (¼ pint) liquid. Cover and stir once during cooking. Allow to stand for about 15 mins.

DRIED PEARS AND APPLE SLICES

Quantity	Cooking time on FULL (in mins)		
	500W	**600W**	700W
100g (4oz)	5-8	**5-8**	5-8

Cooking technique Place in a large dish and add 900ml (1½ pints) of boiling water. Cover and cook. Stir once during cooking then leave to stand for 10-30 mins. Avoid doing more than 100g (4 oz) at one time as they swell enormously during cooking.

Dried pear

Dried apple ring

DRIED DATES

Quantity	Cooking time on FULL (in mins)		
	500W	**600W**	700W
225g (8oz)	4-6	**3-5**	3-5

Cooking technique Place in a dish with 150ml (¼ pint) of boiling water. Cover and cook. Stir once during cooking. Leave to stand for 10-15 mins. Cook with fresh fruit to add sweetness, for example with rhubarb or cooking apples. Alternatively, try them puréed as a spread or use as a sugar substitute when baking.

Dried dates

DRIED BANANAS

Quantity	Cooking time on FULL (in mins)		
	500W	**600W**	700W
225g (8oz)	10-12	**10-12**	10-12

Cooking technique To make an interesting purée or spread, chop the bananas very finely then place in a dish with 600ml (1 pint) boiling water. Cover and cook, stirring once or twice during cooking. Stand until cool, then drain and purée with orange or lemon juice added to taste.

Dried bananas

DRIED FIGS

Quantity	Cooking time on FULL (in mins)		
	500W	**600W**	700W
225g (8oz)	8-10	**8-10**	8-10

Cooking technique Place in a dish and cover with boiling water. Cover and cook. Stir once or twice during cooking. Leave to stand for 30 mins. to soften.

Dried peaches

DRIED PEACHES

Quantity	Cooking time on FULL (in mins)		
	500W	**600W**	700W
100g (4oz)	6-10	**5-8**	5-8

Cooking technique Place in a dish with 600ml (1 pint) of boiling water. Cover and cook, stirring once during cooking. Allow to stand for 10-30 mins.

Prunes

PRUNES

Quantity	Cooking time on FULL (in mins)		
	500W	**600W**	700W
225g (8oz)	10-12	**10-12**	10-12

Cooking technique Place in a dish with 600ml (1 pint) of boiling water. Cover and cook, stirring once or twice during cooking. Leave to stand for 15-30 mins.

Nuts and seeds

With a microwave oven, you can toast nuts and seeds in minutes to enhance their flavour and make tasty toppings, fillings and garnishes. The addition of different spices and seasonings will quickly convert them into delicious savoury snacks, as described below. Nut roasts and nut loaf mixtures cook successfully by microwave. Ensure that the raw mixture is well flavoured and quite moist for the best results. If the finished loaf looks too anaemic for your liking, simply brown it for a few minutes under a conventional grill before serving.

Fresh chestnut

Dried chestnuts

Pumpkin seeds

Sunflower seeds

Pine kernels

Sesame seeds

DRIED CHESTNUTS

Quantity	Cooking time on FULL and MEDIUM/DEFROST (in mins)		
	500W	**600W**	700W
50g (2oz)	6 & 22	**5 & 15**	4 & 12

Cooking technique Steep the chestnuts in boiling water for 1 hour. Cover and cook on FULL for 5 mins. then reduce power and simmer for 15 mins. or until soft.

FRESH CHESTNUTS

Quantity	Cooking time on FULL (in mins)		
	500W	**600W**	700W
50g (2oz)	1-2	**1-2**	½-1

Cooking technique To shell fresh chestnuts, score the outer case of each nut (or they are liable to explode). Place on a flat dish and shake halfway through. If they don't peel easily, cook for a further 10-15 secs.

Almonds

Hazelnuts

NUTS (GENERAL)

Quantity	Cooking time on FULL (in mins)		
	500W	**600W**	700W
100g (4oz)	3-5	**2-3**	2-3

Cooking technique To roast nuts for garnishes and toppings, simply shell, chop and then spread out on a small plate. Cook uncovered and shake or stir the nuts 2 or 3 times to prevent any scorching. Whole nuts and large pieces will take a little longer; try doubling the times. To make savoury nuts, roast as described then add 15-30ml (1-2 tbsp) shoyu. Stir well, then cook for a futher minute. Allow to cool and serve as a snack or as an addition to salads. For further nut recipes and ideas, see p. 45, 51 and 66.

HAZELNUTS AND PEANUTS

Quantity	Cooking time on FULL (in mins)		
	500W	**600W**	700W
50g (2oz)	6-10	**5-8**	3-6

Cooking technique To toast and skin, shell the nuts and put on a small plate. Cook uncovered and stir 3 or 4 times throughout the cooking period. Leave to cool, then place in a clean tea-towel and rub off the skins.

SEEDS (GENERAL)

Quantity	Cooking time on FULL (in mins)		
	500W	**600W**	700W
50g (2oz)	2-4	**2-3**	1-2

Cooking technique Sunflower and pumpkin seeds are delicious plainly toasted or mixed with 15ml (1 tbsp) shoyu and cooked for a further minute to make a savoury snack. Stir frequently during the cooking period to avoid any scorching. You can make gomasio (a nutty condiment from the Far East) by toasting sesame seeds and then grinding them with sea salt in a ratio of 10:1. Sprinkle over foods as a seasoning. Try toasting other seeds too when required in recipes as it always brings out their flavour. Cumin and coriander are particularly good toasted, then mixed with yogurt and served as an accompaniment to rice dishes.

Walnuts

Pecan nuts

Peanuts

Brazil nuts

Cashew nuts

Whole green lentils

Pulses

With the exception of split peas and lentils, all pulses must be soaked for 8 hours before cooking in the microwave. After soaking, drain the beans and rinse them thoroughly before cooking in fresh boiling water. Be sure to use a container large enough to allow for further swelling during cooking and top up with more boiling water if necessary. Because the beans are cooked by the boiling water rather than microwave power, the cooking times are virtually the same for all microwave ovens. Use the times as a guide but remember that they will vary according to the age of the pulses. If they are tough to bite on after their standing time, simply cook for a little longer. Cooked pulses and pulse dishes are excellent reheated in the microwave. Reheat on LOW to prevent them disintegrating.

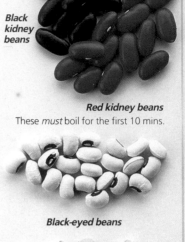
Black kidney beans

Red kidney beans
These *must* boil for the first 10 mins.

WHOLE LENTILS

Quantity	Cooking time on FULL (in mins)		
	500W	**600W**	700W
225g (8oz)	15-20	**15-20**	15-20

Cooking technique Sieve through for grit and stones, rinse and place in a large dish. Cover well with fresh boiling water. Cook covered, stirring 2-3 times. Leave to stand for 10-15 mins. If they are still hard, extend the cooking time and test again.

Aduki beans

ADUKI BEANS

Quantity	Cooking time on FULL (in mins)		
	500W	**600W**	700W
225g (8oz)	25-30	**25-30**	25-30

Cooking technique After soaking, rinse the beans and place them in a large dish. Cover well with fresh boiling water and cook covered. Stir 2 or 3 times during cooking then leave to stand for 15-20 mins. If they are not completely soft, cook for a further 5 mins. and test again.

Mung beans

MUNG BEANS

Quantity	Cooking time on FULL (in mins)		
	500W	**600W**	700W
225g (8oz)	20-25	**20-25**	20-25

Cooking technique Soak the mung beans overnight. Rinse then drain. Put in a large dish and cover with fresh boiling water. Cook covered, stirring 2 or 3 times. Leave to stand for about 10 mins.

Whole green peas

WHOLE GREEN PEAS

Quantity	Cooking time on FULL (in mins)		
	500W	**600W**	700W
225g (8oz)	25-30	**25-30**	25-30

Cooking technique Presoak then rinse and drain. Put in a large dish and cover with fresh boiling water. Cook covered, stirring 2 or 3 times. Leave to stand for 5-10 mins. Test, and extend the cooking time by a further 5 mins. if they are still hard, then test again.

Black-eyed beans

SPLIT PEAS AND RED LENTILS

Quantity	Cooking time on FULL (in mins)		
	500W	**600W**	700W
225g (8oz)	12-15	**10-12**	8-10

Cooking technique Put in a large dish and cover with boiling water. Stand the dish on a plate in case the liquid boils over. Cook covered then allow to stand for 5-10 mins.

Split red lentils

Split green peas

Split yellow peas

ALL LARGER PULSES

Quantity	Cooking time on FULL (in mins)		
	500W	**600W**	700W
225g (8oz)	20-30	**20-30**	20-30

Cooking technique Presoak, rinse and drain. Put in a large dish and cover well with fresh boiling water. Cook covered but ensure that the beans are boiling hard for the first 10 mins. Stir 2 or 3 times during cooking. Leave to stand for 5-10 mins. Cook for a further 5-10 mins. if the pulses are still too hard your liking.

Chick peas

Butter beans

Pinto beans

Flageolet beans

Haricot beans

Mushrooms and seaweeds

Wakame

Dried mushrooms and seaweeds keep indefinitely in the store-cupboard and reconstitute quickly in the microwave with no loss of flavour or nutritional value. Use dried mushrooms to add interesting flavour and texture to soups and vegetable dishes. Seaweed is used as more of a mineral-rich flavouring or seasoning than a vegetable and is only ever required in small quantities, which cook well in the microwave with no risk of the water boiling dry.

Fresh oyster mushrooms

Dulse

Kombu

Fresh button mushrooms

DRIED WAKAME, KOMBU AND ARAME

Quantity	Cooking time on FULL (in mins)		
	500W	**600W**	700W
10g (½oz)	1-2	**1-2**	1-2

Cooking technique To reconstitute, rinse and then cook, covered, in about 200ml (7 fl oz) of boiling water. Drain and mix with vegetables or allow to cool for use in salads. Alternatively, add uncooked to soups, stews and stocks or use as a seasoning for sprinkling over dishes by toasting for 1 min. then grinding with toasted sesame seeds.

DULSE

Quantity	Cooking time on FULL (in mins)		
	500W	**600W**	700W
10g (½oz)	2-3	**2-3**	2-3

Cooking technique Rinse. Cook, covered, in 200ml (7 fl oz) water and 15ml (1 tbsp) shoyu.

Shitake (Dried Chinese mushrooms)

SHITAKE (DRIED CHINESE MUSHROOMS)

Quantity	Cooking time on FULL (in mins)		
	500W	**600W**	700W
25g (1oz)	2-4	**2-3**	1-2

Cooking technique Place in a bowl and cover with boiling water. Cook covered then leave to stand for 10-15 mins. Chop and use in soups, stews and stocks. Retain the rich soaking liquid as it provides extra flavour in stocks and sauces.

FRESH MUSHROOMS

Quantity	Cooking time on FULL (in mins)		
	500W	**600W**	700W
100g (4oz)	3-5	**3-5**	2-4

Cooking technique Select dry, firm mushrooms for use in the microwave and avoid any that are wet, shrivelled or limp. Wipe carefully, then slice or leave whole. Place in a bowl, sprinkle with lemon juice, or dot with butter, and cook. To yield more juice for use in sauces and stocks, cover and cook for 1-2 mins. longer.

Fresh field mushroom

Arame

Grains and cereals

The main advantage of cooking whole grains in the microwave is not the time-saving element, which is minimal, but the fact that the grains remain separate and fluffy. There is also less risk of them burning. Use the standard ratios of water to grain and always add boiling water. Choose large containers as grains treble in size during cooking, and cover loosely so steam can escape. Whole grains reheat successfully in the microwave too, keeping their texture and flavour.

Pot barley

Roasted buckwheat

POT BARLEY

Quantity	Cooking time on FULL (in mins)		
	500W	**600W**	700W
100g (4oz)	20-25	**20-25**	20-25

Cooking technique Place in a large dish and pour over 600ml (1 pint) boiling water. Soak for 1 hour then cook as above stirring 2-3 times. Stand for 10 mins. then drain. For a stronger flavour, roast the grains for 1-2 mins. before adding the water.

Bulgar wheat

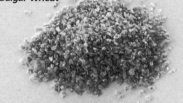

BULGAR WHEAT

Quantity	Cooking time on FULL (in mins)		
	500W	**600W**	700W
100g (4oz)	2-3	**2-3**	2-3

Cooking technique Place in a bowl with 300ml (½ pint) boiling water. Stir well, cover and cook. Stir once during cooking. Allow to stand for 5 mins. then drain and fork through. Season well. Use the same method for COUSCOUS.

POLENTA

Quantity	Cooking time on FULL (in mins)		
	500W	**600W**	700W
100g (4oz)	12-15	**10-12**	8-10

Cooking technique Add 600ml (1 pint) boiling water to the polenta and stir until smooth. Add 25g (1 oz) margarine and mix in. Cover and cook, stirring 4 times. Spoon out onto a greased shallow dish. Stand for 10-15 mins.

Polenta

Brown rice (long grain)

Brown rice (short grain)

BROWN RICE

Quantity	Cooking time on FULL (in mins)		
	500W	**600W**	700W
225g (8oz)	16-20	**16-20**	16-20

Cooking technique Place in a large bowl. Cover well with double the quantity of boiling water. Cover and stir halfway through. Allow to stand for 5-10 mins. then drain. This should result in chewy textured rice.

OATFLAKES AND OATMEAL

Quantity	Cooking time on FULL (in mins)		
	500W	**600W**	700W
50g (2oz)	4-6	**3-5**	2-4

Cooking technique To make porridge for 1 person and serve it in the same container, put the oats into a bowl and cover with 2-3 times their volume of cold water or milk. Stir in well then cover and cook. Stir once or twice during cooking. Leave to stand for 3 mins. Stir again then serve. Follow the same method to make porridge from other flaked grains or a richer, muesli-based mixture.

Oatflakes

Oatmeal

BUCKWHEAT

Quantity	Cooking time on FULL (in mins)		
	500W	**600W**	700W
225g (8oz)	8-10	**8-10**	8-10

Cooking technique Place grains in a large bowl. Add 900ml (1½ pints) boiling water and stir well. Cover and cook, stirring once or twice. Leave to stand for 4-5 mins. Excess water should be absorbed, but drain if necessary.

Whole wheat grains

WHOLE WHEAT

Quantity	Cooking time on FULL (in mins)		
	500W	**600W**	700W
225g (8oz)	25-30	**25-30**	25-30

Cooking technique Cover in boiling water and soak for 1 hour. Drain and add 900ml (1½ pints) of boiling water. Cover and cook, stirring several times. Stand for 15-20 mins. then drain. If grains are not completely soft, cook for a further 5 mins. and test again.

MILLET

Quantity	Cooking time on FULL (in mins)		
	500W	**600W**	700W
50g (2oz)	12-15	**12-15**	12-15

Cooking technique Place grains in a bowl. Add 300ml (½ pint) boiling water. Cover and stir 2-3 times. Stand for 4 mins. to cook through and drain if necessary.

Millet

Pasta

Fresh pasta shapes

Pasta relies on the action of boiling water to soften and cook. As a result, cooking times in the microwave are the same for all models and similar to timings in conventional cookery. The advantages are no messy pans and you can make accompanying sauces while the pasta is standing and cooking through. For the best results, only cook small quantities, no more than 225g (8oz) at a time; always boil the water in a kettle first, pour into a suitable dish and then add the pasta, ensuring that it is totally immersed. The water should cover it to a depth of about 5cm (2 in). Any pieces that protrude will become hard and brittle. All pasta dishes reheat well in the microwave.

Dried spaghetti

Dried pasta shapes

PASTA SHAPES

Dried

Quantity	Cooking time on FULL (in mins)		
	500W	**600W**	700W
225g (8oz)	6-8	**6-8**	6-8

Cooking technique Pour enough boiling water into a dish to completely immerse pasta. Add a little salt and 15ml (1 tbsp) oil. Stir to separate the pasta pieces. Cook uncovered. Allow to stand for 3 mins. then drain and toss in a little olive oil or butter.

Fresh

Quantity	Cooking time on FULL (in mins)		
	500W	**600W**	700W
225g (8oz)	1-3	**1-3**	1-3

Cooking technique Immerse in boiling water and stir. Cook uncovered. Allow to stand for 2 mins. then drain.

EGG AND SPINACH NOODLES

Dried

Quantity	Cooking time on FULL (in mins)		
	500W	**600W**	700W
225g (8oz)	2-5	**2-4**	2-4

Cooking technique Place in a bowl of boiling water and completely immerse. Stir then cook. Stir once during cooking. Allow to stand for 3 mins. then drain.

Dried egg noodles

LASAGNE

Dried

Quantity	Cooking time on FULL (in mins)		
	500W	**600W**	700W
225g (8oz)	8-10	**8-10**	8-10

Cooking technique Place lasagne in a large bowl of boiling water so it is completely immersed. Cook uncovered, stirring once to prevent pieces sticking together. Leave to stand for 5-10 mins. then drain. Fresh and precooked lasagne can be used as they are in dishes as they will soften in the sauce.

Dried spinach noodles

Fresh spinach lasagne

Dried wholemeal spinach lasagne

MACARONI

Dried

Quantity	Cooking time on FULL (in mins)		
	500W	**600W**	700W
225g (8oz)	6-8	**6-8**	6-8

Cooking technique Immerse in a bowl of boiling water. Stir and then cook. Stir once during cooking. Allow to stand for 3 mins. Drain then toss in a little oil or butter.

Dried macaroni

Fresh spaghetti

SPAGHETTI

Dried

Quantity	Cooking time on FULL (in mins)		
	500W	**600W**	700W
225g (8oz)	6-8	**6-8**	6-8

Cooking technique Immerse in boiling water, ensuring that every strand is covered. Add 15ml (1 tbsp) oil and stir. Cook, stirring once, then stand for 5 mins. Drain and toss in a little olive oil or butter.

Fresh

Quantity	Cooking time on FULL (in mins)		
	500W	**600W**	700W
225g (8oz)	1-4	**1-3**	1-3

Cooking technique Immerse in boiling water, separate strands and ensure that none are protruding. Cook uncovered then stand for 3 mins. Drain and then toss in a little olive oil or butter before serving.

Recipe guidelines

Each recipe is supplied with a range of symbols so you can see at a glance how much time you should allow for preparation and cooking, how many servings it will make, whether you can reheat it or freeze it, and whether you should make it in advance.

KEY TO THE SYMBOLS

 The time allowed for preparing the ingredients: measuring, scrubbing, chopping, mixing, blending.

 The total cooking time required in a 600-650W microwave oven.

The power settings used.

This dish reheats well.

 This dish freezes well.

 This dish should be made in advance to allow for chilling times or for the various flavours to blend.

The approximate number of servings. These will depend upon size of appetite and whether the dish is being served as a starter, a side dish or a main course.

(See pages 123-130 for more information on these techniques.)

POINTS TO REMEMBER

The timings in the recipes are for the quantities of food stated. If you alter the amounts, you'll need to adjust the timings accordingly. As a rule, extend the cooking time by a third to a half again when doubling the amount and reduce when cooking less.

Notice that ingredients are given in both metric and imperial measures. Use one system or the other, don't mix the two.

Follow the recipe instructions for covering, piercing, stirring and rearranging. (See pages 123-130 for more information on these techniques.) Never cover dishes so they are completely airtight.

Follow any recipe instructions on the size and type of container. Use smaller ones when reducing amounts.

Always leave the food to stand for the time specified as this is an essential part of the cooking process.

Use oven gloves when removing containers from the microwave as they absorb heat from cooked foods.

Always consult the manufacturer's instruction manual when in any doubt.

COMPARISON OF POWER OUTPUTS USED IN RECIPES

The wattage of your microwave oven determines how long different foods take to cook. All the recipes in this book give timings for 600W (700W and 500W) ovens respectively. Occasionally you'll see that timings are the same for all powers either because they are so short or because of the food type. However, as microwave ovens vary appreciably from one manufacturer to another and even from one model to another, you may need to adapt some of the timings slightly to suit your own oven's cooking characteristics.

The chart below shows the power settings employed to test the following recipes as well as some of the descriptions used by different manufacturers. Use it as a guide in conjunction with your oven's instruction manual. Reduce timings slightly for higher wattages and extend them for lower ones.

Description on 700W and 600-650W oven	Keep warm	**Low**	Stew	**Medium**	Bake	**Medium-High**	**Full**
500W oven	Warm	**Defrost**		Simmer	Roast	Reheat	**Full**
% power output	20%	**25-30%**	40%	**50%**	60-70%	**75-80%**	**100%**
Approximate power output							
700W oven	140W	**170-210W**	280W	**350W**	420-450W	**525-550W**	**700W**
600-650W oven	100-150W	**150-200W**	250W	**300W**	370-400W	**435-470W**	**600-650W**
500W oven	100W	**125-175W**	200W	255W	300-350%	375-400W	**500W**

Figures in bold = *settings used in* R E C I P E S

RECIPES

Each of the following recipes has been tested in a range of ovens and cooking times are supplied for machines with 500W, 600W and 700W power outputs throughout. The recommended timings and instructions are as accurate as I can make them but may need adapting according to the condition and size of your ingredients, the shape and type of container and the make of oven you use. Note the recipe guidelines and explanations opposite, and play safe by cooking foods for the minimum time stated then adding a little extra time after testing if required.

If you are new to microwave cookery, read pages 113-139 for a better understanding of basic microwave facts and cooking techniques. Try a few simple recipes to start with, note any adjustments that you need to make, then gradually increase your repertoire. Remember you can vary ingredients in recipes according to what you have available, using the charts on pages 10-27 as a guide.

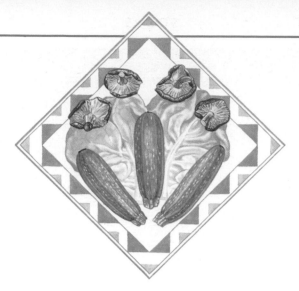

SOUPS

Soups cooked in the microwave retain the full flavour, colour and nutritional value of their ingredients while conserving your energy both in terms of cooking time and washing up. All soups can be made in the bowl in which they are to be served and there is no danger of thicker soups catching and sticking to the bottom as when cooked over direct heat. Use a large, round, deep container which will accomodate any liquid expansion and facilitate stirring. Chop vegetables into small, even-sized pieces and always use a hot liquid base to speed up the cooking process. Soups containing a mixture of fresh and dried ingredients benefit by being cooked in advance and left to stand for several hours so that the flavours have time to blend together. Reheat just before serving: an individual portion will take between 3 and 5 minutes in a bowl or mug. Stir once or twice during this time to ensure even heat distribution.

Chestnut and tomato soup

INGREDIENTS

| 50g (2 oz) dried chestnuts |
| 600ml (1 pint) boiling water |
| 10ml (2 tsp) sunflower oil |
| 1 medium onion, finely chopped |
| 225g (8 oz) carrots, diced |
| 2 bay leaves |
| 400g (14 oz) can tomatoes |
| 15-30ml (1-2 tbsp) tomato purée |
| 5-10ml (1-2 tsp) shoyu |
| salt and black pepper |
| **Garnish** |
| fresh parsley |

The sweet flavour of the chestnuts blends well with the carrots, and together they balance any acidity in the tomatoes.

1   Put the chestnuts in a medium bowl and pour over the boiling water. Leave to soak for 1 hour, then cover and ≋ FULL for 5 mins. 600W *(4 mins. 700W; 6 mins. 500W)* until boiling, then ≋ MEDIUM for 15 mins. 600W *(12-13 mins. 700W; ≋ DEFROST for 22 mins. 500W)* or until tender, stirring several times. Leave to stand for 5 mins. then drain, reserving the stock.

2   Put the oil in a medium dish and ≋ FULL for 1 min. 600W *(30 secs. 700W; 1 min. 500W)*. Stir in the onion, then ≋ FULL for 2 mins. 600W *(1½ mins. 700W; 2½ mins. 500W)*.

3   Add the carrots, chestnuts and bay leaves. Cover and ≋ FULL for 3 mins. 600W *(2½ mins. 700W; 3½ mins. 500W)*.

4   Add the tomatoes, tomato purée and 300ml (½ pint) of the chestnut stock. Re-cover and ≋ FULL for 10 mins. 600W *(8½ mins. 700W; 12½ mins. 500W)*, stirring several times.

5   Cool slightly, remove the bay leaves, then liquidize, adding a little more stock if necessary. Season well with shoyu, salt and pepper. To reheat, cover and ≋ FULL for 1-2 mins. then garnish with parsley before serving.

★ **Preparation:**
15 minutes, plus 1 hour soaking

≋ **Cooking time:**
37 minutes

⊘ **Power settings:**
FULL and MEDIUM

≋ **Good reheated**

◎ **Serves 4-6**

★ If you don't have time to soak the chestnuts, you can cook them from dried. Cover with plenty of boiling water and ≋ FULL for 10 mins. *(all powers)*. Continue ≋ MEDIUM for 20-25 mins. 600W *(and 700W; ≋ FULL for 20-25 mins. 500W.)*

Illustrated opposite

Top: **Onion and cider soup** *(see p. 32)*; Bottom: **Chestnut and tomato soup** *(see above)*

Onion and cider soup

INGREDIENTS

15ml (1 tbsp) sunflower oil
350g (12 oz) onions, thinly sliced
2 cloves garlic, crushed
300ml (½ pint) boiling vegetable stock
300ml (½ pint) medium dry cider
5ml (1 tsp) chopped fresh sage
5ml (1 tsp) mustard powder
15-30ml (1-2 tbsp) shoyu
15ml (1 tbsp) miso, dissolved in a little water
For the topping
15ml (1 tbsp) olive oil
40g (1½ oz) wholemeal breadcrumbs
25g (1 oz) chopped nuts
2.5ml (½ tsp) mustard powder

This tasty version of French onion soup has a delicious crunchy topping in place of the traditional toasted slice of French bread with Gruyère cheese. Alternatively, serve with croûtons.

1 Put the oil in a medium dish and ≋ FULL for 1 min. 600W *(30 secs. 700W; 1 min. 500W)*. Stir in the onions and ≋ FULL for 2 mins. 600W *(1½ mins. 700W; 2½ mins. 500W)*.

2 Add the garlic, cover and ≋ FULL for 2 mins. 600W *(1½ mins. 700W; 2½ mins. 500W)*.

3 Add the stock, cider, seasonings and shoyu and ≋ FULL for 5 mins. 600W *(4 mins. 700W; 6 mins. 500W)*, then ≋ MEDIUM for 10 mins. 600W *(8 mins. 700W; ≋ DEFROST for 15 mins. 500W)*, stirring once or twice.

4 Add the miso to the soup and ≋ MEDIUM for 1 min. 600W *(30 secs. 700W; ≋ DEFROST for 1½ mins. 500W)*.

5 For the topping, put the oil in a medium dish and ≋ FULL for 1 min. 600W *(30 secs. 700W; 1 min. 500W)*. Stir in the breadcrumbs, nuts and mustard powder until well coated with hot oil. ≋ FULL for 2 mins. 600W *(1½ mins. 700W; 2½ mins. 500W)*. Sprinkle over the soup, either in the serving dish or in individual bowls. Reheat for 1-2 mins. before serving if necessary.

 Preparation: 20 minutes

Cooking time: 24 minutes

 Power settings: FULL and MEDIUM

Serves 4

★ To make croûtons, heat 15ml (1 tbsp) oil for 1 min. Add 50g (2 oz) small bread cubes and stir. ≋ FULL for 2 mins. 600W *(1½ mins. 700W; 2½ mins. 500W)*, stirring halfway through. Cover and allow to stand for 2 mins. before using.

Illustrated on p. 31

Cream of lettuce soup

INGREDIENTS

600ml (1 pint) skimmed milk
½ medium onion
1 bay leaf
6 peppercorns
15ml (1 tbsp) sunflower oil
3 spring onions, trimmed and chopped
1 clove garlic, crushed
2.5ml (½ tsp) celery seeds
2.5ml (½ tsp) grated nutmeg
1 large crisp or flat lettuce, shredded
Garnish
chopped spring onion tops or chives

To make a good lettuce soup, you need a well flavoured milk base or stock. It's quick and easy to infuse milk in the microwave using a measuring jug, but do ensure that it is large enough to allow for any liquid expansion.

1 Put the milk, onion, bay leaf and peppercorns in a large jug or bowl and ≋ FULL for 4 mins. 600W *(3 mins. 700W; 5 mins. 500W)*. Leave to stand for 3 mins. then strain.

2 Put the oil in a medium dish and ≋ FULL for 1 min. 600W *(30 secs. 700W; 1 min. 500W)*. Stir in the onions, garlic, celery seeds and nutmeg. Cover and ≋ FULL for 1½ mins. 600W *(1 min. 700W; 1½ mins. 500W)*.

3 Stir in the shredded lettuce, re-cover and ≋ FULL for 3 mins. 600W *(2½ mins. 700W; 3½ mins. 500W)*.

4 Pour in the infused milk, then liquidize.

5 Return the soup to the dish, cover and ≋ FULL for 1-2 mins. to reheat.

6 Garnish with chopped spring onion tops or chives.

★ **Preparation:** 15 minutes

Cooking time: 10½ minutes

Power setting: FULL

Good reheated

Serves 4

 Warmed bread rolls are always delicious with soup. To heat them through, place in the oven and ≋ FULL for about 30 secs.

Illustrated opposite

Top: **Borsch** *(see p. 35)*; Centre: **Oriental mushroom soup** *(see p. 35)*; Bottom: **Cream of lettuce soup** *(see above)*

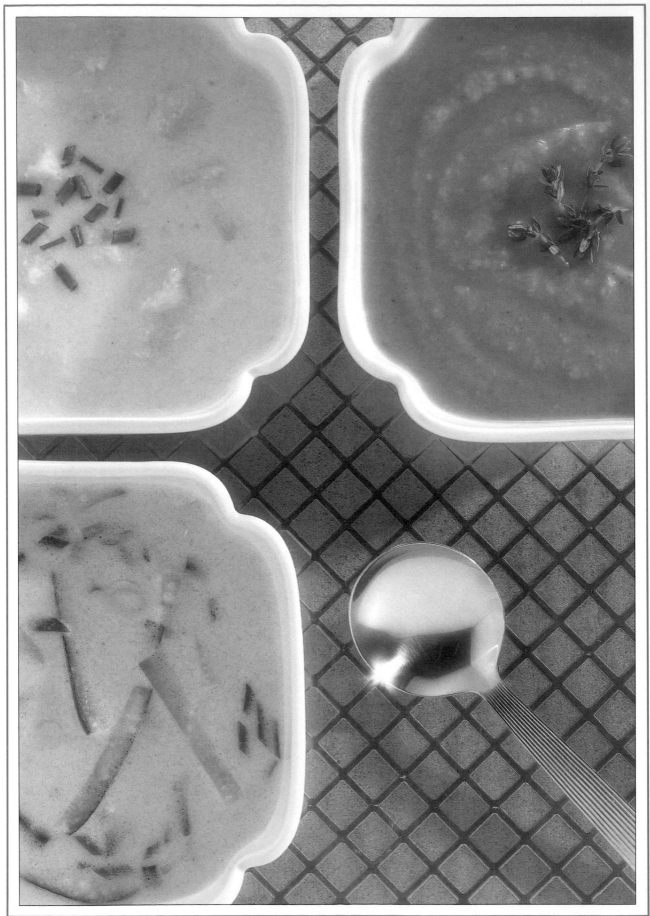

Oriental mushroom soup

INGREDIENTS

8 dried shitake mushrooms
300ml (½ pint) boiling water
15ml (1 tbsp) groundnut oil
50g (2 oz) shallots, chopped
2.5ml (½ tsp) grated fresh root ginger
175g (6 oz) button mushrooms, wiped and thinly sliced
100g (4 oz) carrots, sliced into thin rings
7.5g (¼ oz) arame seaweed
450ml (¾ pint) boiling vegetable stock
15-30ml (1-2 tbsp) shoyu
15ml (1 tbsp) sherry

Dried mushrooms are an invaluable ingredient for adding extra flavour and texture. The microwave speeds up the process of reconstituting them, making this recipe extremely quick.

1   Put the mushrooms in a medium dish and pour over the boiling water. Cover and ≈ FULL for about 2 mins. *(all powers)*. Leave to soak for 10-15 mins, then slice the mushrooms and reserve the water.

2   Put the oil in a medium dish and ≈ FULL for 1 min. 600W *(30 secs. 700W; 1 min. 500W)*. Add the shallots and grated root ginger, stir well, then ≈ FULL for 2 mins. 600W *(1½ mins. 700W; 2½ mins. 500W)*.

3   Add the dried and button mushrooms and the carrots. Cover and ≈ FULL for 2 mins. 600W *(1½ mins. 700W; 2½ mins. 500W)*, stirring once or twice.

4   Add the seaweed, stock, mushroom water, shoyu and sherry. Re-cover and ≈ FULL for 3-4 mins. 600W *(2-3 mins. 700W; 4-5 mins. 500W)*.

5   Leave to stand for 5 mins, then season to taste and serve.

★ **Preparation:**
20 minutes

≈ **Cooking time:**
10 minutes

⊘ **Power setting:**
FULL

≈ **Good reheated**

◎ **Serves 4**

Illustrated on p.33

Borsch

INGREDIENTS

15ml (1 tbsp) sunflower oil
1 small onion, finely chopped
2 sticks celery, diced
1 medium carrot, diced
1 medium parsnip, diced
225g (8 oz) uncooked beetroot, diced
200g (7 oz) can tomatoes, puréed
10ml (2 tsp) caraway seeds
15ml (1 tbsp) dill weed
45ml (3 tbsp) fresh parsley
300ml (½ pint) boiling vegetable stock
juice of ½ lemon
salt and black pepper
For serving
natural yogurt

This microwave version of borsch is quick to make, and the flavour has all the freshness of raw vegetables.

1   Put the oil in a large bowl and ≈ FULL for 1 min. 600W *(30 secs. 700W; 1 min. 500W)*.

2   Stir in the chopped onion and celery, then ≈ FULL for 2 mins. 600W *(1½ mins. 700W; 2½ mins. 500W)*, stirring once during cooking.

3   Add the carrot, parsnip, beetroot, puréed tomatoes, caraway seeds, chopped herbs and boiling stock. Cover and ≈ FULL for 7 mins. 600W *(6 mins. 700W; 8½ mins. 500W)*.

3   Cool slightly, then liquidize to make either a textured or smooth consistency.

4   Add lemon juice to taste, then season well with salt and pepper. Chill thoroughly.

5   Add a swirl of yogurt just before serving.

★ **Preparation:**
20 minutes, plus chilling

≈ **Cooking time:**
10 minutes

⊘ **Power setting:**
FULL

≈ **Make in advance**

◎ **Serves 4**

Illustrated on p. 33

Top left: **Cream of garlic soup** *(see p. 36)*; Top right: **Yellow split pea and parsnip soup** *(see p. 36)*; Bottom left: **Courgette soup julienne** *(see p. 36)*

Cream of garlic soup

INGREDIENTS

15ml (1 tbsp) olive oil
1 head garlic (10-12 cloves), crushed
225g (8 oz) parsnips, diced
600ml (1 pint) boiling stock
4 eggs
10-15ml (2-3 tsp) vinegar
salt and black pepper

Despite the large amount of garlic, this creamy soup has a delicious, subtle flavour and is extremely quick to make.

1   Put the oil in a medium dish and ≋ FULL for 1 min. 600W *(30 secs. 700W; 1 min. 500W)*. Add the garlic and ≋ MEDIUM for 2 mins. 600W *(1½ mins. 700W; ≋ DEFROST for 3 mins. 500W)*.

2   Add the parsnips and boiling stock, cover and ≋ MEDIUM for 6 mins. 600W *(5 mins. 700W; ≋ DEFROST for 9 mins. 500W)*, stirring once or twice.

3   In a separate bowl, beat the eggs with the vinegar, then whisk into the soup. Re-cover and ≋ MEDIUM for a further 2 mins. 600W *(1½ mins. 700W; ≋ DEFROST for 3 mins. 500W)*, whisking halfway through. Season well and serve.

★ **Preparation:**
10 minutes

≋ **Cooking time:**
11 minutes

▨ **Power settings:**
FULL AND MEDIUM

≋ **Good reheated**

◉ **Serves 4**

≋ Reheat on LOW or DEFROST to prevent the mixture from curdling.

Illustrated on p. 34

Yellow split pea and parsnip soup

INGREDIENTS

15ml (1 tbsp) sunflower oil
1 onion, finely chopped
1 clove garlic, crushed
225g (8 oz) parsnips, diced
2 sticks celery, diced
30ml (2 tbsp) chopped fresh parsley
5ml (1 tsp) fresh thyme
100g (4 oz) yellow split peas
450ml (¾ pint) boiling vegetable stock
5ml (1 tsp) miso
salt and black pepper

A warming soup for cold winter evenings.

1   Put the oil in a medium dish and ≋ FULL for 1 min. 600W *(30 secs. 700W; 1 min. 500W)*. Stir in the onion and garlic and ≋ FULL for 1 min. 600W *(30 secs. 700W; 1 min. 500W)*.

2   Add the parsnips, celery and herbs, cover and ≋ FULL for 3 mins. 600W *(2½ mins. 700W; 3½ mins. 500W)*.

3   Add the split peas and stock, re-cover and ≋ FULL for 30 mins. 600W *(25 mins. 700W; 37 mins. 500W)*, stirring several times.

4   Cool slightly, then liquidize until smooth. Stir in the miso, dissolved in a little water, and season to taste.

5   Return the soup to the dish, cover and ≋ FULL for 1-2 mins. to reheat. Serve with croûtons or warmed wholemeal rolls.

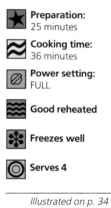

★ **Preparation:**
25 minutes

≋ **Cooking time:**
36 minutes

▨ **Power setting:**
FULL

≋ **Good reheated**

❋ **Freezes well**

◉ **Serves 4**

Illustrated on p. 34

Courgette soup julienne

INGREDIENTS

450ml (¾ pint) skimmed milk
½ medium onion
1 bay leaf
1 sprig fresh parsley
2.5ml (½ tsp) dill seed
2.5ml (½ tsp) peppercorns
15ml (1 tbsp) sunflower oil
4 spring onions, trimmed and chopped
1 clove garlic, crushed
225g (8 oz) courgettes, cut into julienne strips
15ml (1 tbsp) rice flour
salt and black pepper

A wonderful creamy soup thickened with a little rice flour, which keeps the mixture light. The milk needs to be infused so that the soup has a full flavour.

1   Put the milk, onion, herbs and spices in a 600ml jug (1 pint) jug and ≋ FULL for 3½ mins. 600W *(3 mins. 700W; 4 mins. 500W)*. Leave to stand for 5 mins, then strain.

2   Put the oil in a medium dish and ≋ FULL for 1 min. 600W *(30 secs. 700W; 1 min. 500W)*. Stir in the spring onions and garlic. ≋ FULL for 2 mins. 600W *(1½ mins. 700W; 2½ mins. 500W)*.

3   Add the courgette strips, cover and ≋ FULL for 4 mins. 600W *(3 mins. 700W; 5 mins. 500W)*, stirring once or twice.

4   Stir in the flour and ≋ FULL for 1 min. 600W *(30 secs. 700W; 1 min. 500W)*.

5   Gradually add the infused milk, cover and ≋ MEDIUM for 5 mins. 600W *(4 mins. 700W; DEFROST for 7 mins. 500W)*, stirring 2-3 times. Season to taste and serve hot.

★ **Preparation:**
15 minutes

≋ **Cooking time:**
16½ minutes

▨ **Power settings:**
FULL and MEDIUM

≋ **Good reheated**

◉ **Serves 4**

Illustrated on p. 34

STARTERS

With a microwave, you can prepare mouthwatering starters well in advance of a dinner party and reheat them moments before serving without any fear of them spoiling or drying out. Vegetables and fruit can be mixed in unusual combinations and cooked quickly so they retain their full flavour, texture and colour. Pâtés and dips will remain moist whether served hot or cold. In addition to the recipes here, you will find many dishes in other sections of the book that can be scaled down and adapted to make appetizing first courses.

Mushrooms stuffed with garlic vegetables

INGREDIENTS
4 large field mushrooms
For the filling
15ml (1 tbsp) olive oil
3 spring onions, trimmed and diced
2 cloves garlic, crushed
1 courgette, diced
5ml (1 tsp) dried oregano
30ml (2 tbsp) tomato purée
5ml (1 tsp) shoyu
salt and black pepper

Choose large field mushrooms as their broad caps make a shallow shell and are easy to stuff. Chop the filling ingredients finely, so that they bind together with the tomato purée.

1   Wipe the mushrooms carefully. Remove the stalks and some of the centre to form a shell. Chop the stalks finely.

2   Put the oil in a medium dish and ≋ FULL for 1 min. 600W *(30 secs. 700W; 1 min. 500W)*. Stir in the onions and garlic and ≋ FULL for 2 mins. 600W *(1½ mins. 700W; 2½ mins. 500W)*, stirring halfway through.

3   Add the chopped mushroom stalks and all the remaining ingredients, except the whole mushrooms and seasoning. Cover and ≋ FULL for 4 mins. 600W *(3 mins. 700W; 5 mins. 500W)*, stirring once.

4   Season the filling to taste with salt and pepper, then pile it into the mushroom caps. Place in a shallow dish, cover and ≋ FULL for 4 mins. 600W *(3 mins. 700W; 5 mins. 500W)*, rearranging halfway through.

5   Leave to stand for 2-3 mins. before serving.

★ **Preparation:**
15 minutes

≋ **Cooking time:**
11 minutes

⊘ **Power setting:**
FULL

◎ **Serves 4**

Illustrated on p. 38

Lentil and coconut pâté

INGREDIENTS

100g (4 oz) split red lentils
400ml (14 fl oz) boiling water
50g (2 oz) creamed coconut, grated
juice of ½ lemon
4-5 drops Tabasco sauce
1.25ml (¼ tsp) grated nutmeg
salt and black pepper

This makes a delicious creamy pâté with a subtle flavour. Red lentils are particularly quick in the microwave, but be sure to cook them in a large bowl or the cooking liquid will froth over the top. Serve the pâté with crudités or Melba toast.

1 Place the red lentils in a deep bowl and pour over the boiling water. Cover and ≈ FULL for 10 mins. *(all powers)*, stirring several times. Drain well, if necessary, reserving any liquid.

2 Stir in the creamed coconut, lemon juice, Tabasco sauce and nutmeg. Liquidize until smooth, adding a little of the reserved lentil stock, or water, if necessary.

3 Season to taste with salt and pepper, then chill thoroughly before serving.

 Preparation:
10 minutes, plus chilling

Cooking time:
10 minutes

Power setting:
FULL

Make in advance

Serves 4

Illustrated opposite

Coriander ramekins

INGREDIENTS

3 eggs
150ml (¼ pint) yogurt
45ml (3 tbsp) chopped fresh coriander
salt and black pepper

If fresh coriander is unavailable, try using mixtures of other fresh herbs, such as chives, parsley or tarragon, or chopped spinach, sorrel or cooked leeks.

1 Beat the eggs thoroughly, then beat in the yogurt. Fold in the coriander, and season to taste with salt and pepper.

2 Spoon the mixture into four ramekin dishes. Cover, then arrange the dishes in a circle in the microwave and ≈ FULL for 3 mins. 600W *(2½ mins. 700W; 3 mins. 500W)*, rearranging halfway through.

3 Leave to stand for 3 mins. before serving.

Preparation:
5 minutes

Cooking time:
3 minutes

Power setting:
FULL

Serves 4

These should be quite soft when served; if overcooked they become rubbery in texture.

Illustrated opposite

Aubergine dip

INGREDIENTS

1 large aubergine
10ml (2 tsp) sesame seeds
10ml (2 tsp) sunflower seeds
30ml (2 tbsp) olive oil
2 cloves garlic, crushed
juice of ½ lemon
2.5ml (½ tsp) ground coriander
salt and black pepper

Aubergines cook very quickly in the microwave, saving time and the need to heat an entire oven simply to make this tasty dip. Choose aubergines that feel heavy for their size and have smooth, glossy skins.

1 Trim the aubergine, then pierce the skin. Wrap in absorbent paper and ≈ FULL for 5 mins. 600W *(4 mins. 700W; 6 mins. 500W)*, turning once. Leave to stand for 4 mins.

2 Spread out the seeds on a small plate and ≈ FULL for 3 mins. 600W *(2½ mins. 700W; 3½ mins. 500W)*, shaking halfway through. Crush lightly.

3 Scoop out the aubergine flesh, mash well and mix with the oil, garlic, lemon juice and coriander. Season well with salt and pepper, then stir in the crushed, toasted seeds. Serve warm as a dip with crudités or strips of toast, or serve as a spread.

 Preparation:
10 minutes

Cooking time:
8 minutes

Power setting:
FULL

Make in advance

Serves 4

 Wrapping aubergines in absorbent paper prevents them collapsing during the cooking process.

Illustrated opposite

Clockwise from Top left: **Lentil and coconut pâté** *(see above);* **Aubergine dip** *(see above);* **Mushrooms stuffed with garlic vegetables** *(see p. 37);* **Coriander ramekins** *(see above)*

Hot melon salad

INGREDIENTS

50g (2 oz) dried apricots
600ml (1 pint) boiling water
2 Ogen or small Gallia melons
1 orange, peeled and segmented
15g (½ oz) stem ginger, diced
30-45ml (2-3 tbsp) white wine
10ml (2 tsp) arrowroot

This fruit cocktail makes an unusual hot and refreshing starter. Serve immediately the fruit is cooked as the mixture starts to cool quite quickly.

1　Put the apricots in a medium dish, pour over the boiling water, cover and ≋ FULL for 4 mins. 600W *(3 mins. 700W; 5 mins. 500W)*, then ≋ MEDIUM for 6 mins. 600W *(5 mins. 700W; ≋ DEFROST for 9 mins. 500W)*. Leave to soak for 30 mins, then chop the apricots and reserve the water.

2　Meanwhile slice the melons in half and discard the seeds. Scoop out the flesh using a melon baller.

3　Mix the melon balls with the apricots, orange and ginger. Drain off the juice into a measuring jug and make up to 200ml (7 fl oz) with the white wine and apricot cooking liquor.

4　Dissolve the arrowroot in 30ml (2 tbsp) of the liquid. Keep the remaining liquid in the jug and ≋ FULL for 2 mins. 600W *(1½ mins. 700W; 2½ mins. 500W)*, then add the dissolved arrowroot and ≋ FULL for 2-3 mins. 600W *(1½-2½ mins. 700W; 2½-3½ mins. 500W)*, stirring once or twice.

5　Divide the fruit between the melon halves and top with sauce. Place in a shallow dish, cover and ≋ FULL for 4 mins. 600W *(3 mins. 700W; 5 mins. 500W)* or until fairly warm, rearranging halfway through. Serve immediately.

★ **Preparation:**
25 minutes, plus 30 minutes soaking

≋ **Cooking time:**
18 minutes

∅ **Power settings:**
FULL and MEDIUM

◎ **Serves 4**

Illustrated below

Leek vinaigrette

INGREDIENTS

450g (1 lb) young leeks, trimmed weight
90ml (6 tbsp) olive oil
30ml (2 tbsp) lemon juice
15ml (1 tbsp) cider vinegar
10ml (2 tsp) capers
5ml (1 tsp) coarse-grained mustard
1 clove garlic, crushed
salt and black pepper

Vegetables cooked in the microwave retain a crisp, fresh flavour and are excellent served chilled in vinaigrette. The same recipe can be used for artichoke hearts, mushrooms or French beans.

1   Chop the leeks into 2.5cm (1 in) pieces and wash thoroughly.

2   Arrange in a dish with 30ml (2 tbsp) water. Cover and ≋ FULL for 4 mins. 600W *(3 mins. 700W; 5 mins. 500W)*, shaking the dish once or twice during cooking. Drain well.

3   Combine all the remaining ingredients, except the seasoning, and add to the cooked leeks. Cover and ≋ FULL for 1 min. 600W *(30 secs. 700W; 1 min. 500W).*

4   Leave to cool completely. Season well with salt and pepper, then chill thoroughly. Delicious served with brown bread or a crisp green salad.

★ **Preparation:** 15 minutes, plus chilling

≋ **Cooking time:** 5 minutes

⊘ **Power setting:** FULL

▦ **Make in advance**

◎ **Serves 4**

Illustrated below

Far left: **Stuffed avocados** *(see p. 42)*; Centre left: **Leek vinaigrette** *(see above)*; Centre right: **Hot melon salad** *(see above, left)*; Far right: **Mung dhal** *(see p. 42)*

Stuffed avocados

INGREDIENTS

25g (1 oz) raisins
juice of 1 orange
50g (2 oz) short-grain brown rice
300ml (½ pint) boiling water
25g (1 oz) sunflower seeds
3 spring onions, finely chopped
5ml (1 tsp) shoyu
5ml (1 tsp) grated fresh root ginger
2 avocados

Hot stuffed avocado makes an unusual alternative to the standard avocado vinaigrette. The microwave heats up the avocado halves without drying them out or making them bitter.

1   Put the raisins in a small bowl, pour over the orange juice and ≋ FULL for 1 min. 600W *(30 secs. 700W; 1 min. 500W)* to plump them up.

2   Put the rice in a medium dish with the boiling water. Cover and ≋ FULL for 18 mins. *(all powers)*, stirring 2-3 times. Leave to stand for 5 mins.

3   Spread out the sunflower seeds on a small plate and ≋ FULL for 2 mins. 600W *(1½ mins. 700W; 2½ mins. 500W)*, shaking halfway through.

4   Mix the raisins, cooked rice, toasted seeds, onions, shoyu and root ginger together.

5   Halve the avocados, scoop out the flesh and dice. Mix the flesh with the other ingredients, then spoon into each of the avocado halves.

6   Arrange the halves in a large round dish with the thicker ends outwards. Cover and ≋ FULL for 2 mins. 600W *(1½ mins. 700W; 2½ mins. 500W)*. Serve at once.

 Preparation: 20 minutes

Cooking time: 23 minutes

Power setting: FULL

Serves 4

 To get more juice from oranges and lemons, microwave individually for 30 secs. before squeezing.

Illustrated on p. 40

Mung dhal

INGREDIENTS

100g (4 oz) mung beans, soaked overnight
600ml (1 pint) boiling water
30ml (2 tbsp) sunflower oil
1 medium onion, finely chopped
1 clove garlic, crushed
1cm (½ in) piece fresh root ginger, grated
5ml (1 tsp) cumin seeds
2.5ml (½ tsp) turmeric
5ml (1 tsp) garam masala
225 (8 oz) courgettes, grated
juice of ½ lemon

These small beans cook quite quickly, as long as you start with boiling water. Don't expect them to mash down in quite the same way as they would if cooked conventionally—the texture is a little firmer and more floury. The grated courgette adds a marvellous quality to the mixture.

1   Drain the mung beans, put in a deep dish and pour over the boiling water. Cover and ≋ FULL for 20 mins. *(all powers)* stirring 2-3 times. Drain, reserving the liquid, then mash.

2   Put the oil in a medium dish and ≋ FULL for 1½ mins. 600W *(1 min. 700W; 1½ mins. 500W)*. Stir in the onion, garlic, ginger and cumin seeds, then ≋ FULL for 1½ mins. 600W *(1 min. 700W; 1½ mins. 500W)*.

3   Add the turmeric, garam masala and grated courgette and mix well. Cover and ≋ FULL for 2 mins. 600W *(1½ mins. 700W; 2½ mins. 500W)*.

4   Add the mashed mung beans with 15-30ml (1-2 tbsp) of the reserved bean stock. Cover and ≋ FULL for 9 mins. 600W *(7½ mins. 700W; 11 mins. 500W)*, stirring 3-4 times. Add the lemon juice and season well. Leave to cool slightly but serve warm.

Preparation: 20 minutes

Cooking time: 34 minutes

Power setting: FULL

Good reheated

Serves 4

 To make Melba toast, toast a slice of bread on both sides then cut in half horizontally to make 2 thinner slices. Place in the microwave untoasted slice up and ≋ FULL for about 30 secs. until crisp and curled.

Illustrated on p. 41

MAIN COURSE DISHES

A wide variety of delicious, nutritious savoury dishes cook well in the microwave. For many recipes, the grains and pulses required can be prepared in advance and then reheated without spoiling. When making casseroles and bakes remember that the speed of cooking does not give the various flavours as much time to develop as in conventional cooking. If possible, make these dishes ahead of time and then reheat them in a covered dish before serving. Dishes such as moussaka and lasagne work very well in the microwave with the added bonus that you can prepare the different layers without creating a pile of dirty dishes. Nut roasts and savoury bakes are also very quick to make and remain moist and flavoursome. Apart from the dishes described here, you can create some wonderful main meals by following recipes from other sections of the book and serving them with pasta, grains or baked potatoes.

Polenta with tomato sauce

INGREDIENTS

100g (4 oz) cornmeal or maize flour
2.5ml (½ tsp) salt
600ml (1 pint) boiling water
25g (1 oz) margarine or butter
For the sauce
15ml (1 tbsp) olive oil
1 medium onion, finely chopped
1 clove garlic, crushed
1 medium green pepper, deseeded and very finely chopped
2 sticks celery, finely chopped
400g (14 oz) can tomatoes, mashed
15-30ml (1-2 tbsp) tomato purée
5ml (1 tsp) miso, dissolved in a little water
1 bay leaf
5ml (1 tsp) dried oregano
salt and black pepper

Polenta is easy to make in a microwave, and it is unlikely to stick or burn. For a more substantial meal, reheat the polenta in a tomato sauce with sliced vegetables such as courgettes, mushrooms or cauliflower florets.

1   Mix the cornmeal and salt together. Stir in the boiling water to make a smooth liquid, then stir in the margarine or butter.

2   Pour the mixture into a medium dish, cover and ≋ FULL for 10 mins. 600W *(8½ mins. 700W; 12½ mins. 500W).*

3   Spoon out onto a greased shallow dish and leave the polenta to set for 10-15 mins.

4   For the sauce, put the oil in a medium dish and ≋ FULL for 1 min. 600W *(30 secs. 700W; 1 min. 500W).* Stir in the onion and garlic and ≋ FULL for 2 mins. 600W *(1½ mins. 700W; 2½ mins. 500W).*

5   Add the pepper and celery, cover and ≋ FULL for 2 mins. 600W *(1½ mins. 700W; 2½ mins. 500W).*

6   Add all the remaining ingredients, except the seasoning, re-cover and ≋ FULL for 7 mins. 600W *(6 mins. 700W; 8½ mins. 500W),* stirring well. Remove the bay leaf and season.

7   Slice the polenta into cubes and place in a shallow dish. Pour over the tomato sauce, cover and ≋ MEDIUM-HIGH for 3-4 mins. 600W *(3 mins. 700W; ≋ FULL for 3 mins. 500W).*

★ **Preparation:**
25 minutes

≋ **Cooking time:**
25 minutes

⊘ **Power settings:**
FULL and MEDIUM-HIGH

≋ **Good reheated**

◎ **Serves 4**

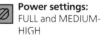

★ The texture of the polenta is soft; for a crisp version, coat in cornmeal and fry conventionally before reheating in the sauce.

Illustrated on p. 44

Millet and mushroom bake

INGREDIENTS

50g (2 oz) millet
300ml (½ pint) boiling water
30ml (2 tbsp) sunflower oil
100g (4 oz) leeks, trimmed and diced
225g (8 oz) mushrooms, diced
225g (8 oz) Jerusalem artichokes, diced
30ml (2 tbsp) chopped fresh parsley
10ml (2 tsp) chopped fresh rosemary
30ml (2 tbsp) wholewheat flour
150ml (¼ pint) milk
salt and black pepper
For the crust
225g (8 oz) self-raising wholewheat flour
2.5ml (½ tsp) salt
50g (2oz) solid vegetable fat
150ml (¼ pint) milk

Vegetarian suet pastry does work in the microwave, but it should be eaten straight away rather than reheated as the pastry tends to harden once it has cooled down.

1   Put the millet in a deep bowl and pour over the boiling water. Cover and ≋ FULL for 12 mins. *(all powers)* stirring 2-3 times. Leave to stand for 4 mins. then drain if necessary.

2   Put the oil in a medium dish and ≋ FULL for 1 min. 600W *(30 secs. 700W; 1 min. 500W)*. Add the leeks, stir well, then ≋ FULL for 2 mins. 600W *(1½ mins. 700W; 2½ mins. 500W)*, stirring once.

3   Add the mushrooms, artichokes and herbs. Stir well then cover and ≋ FULL for 4 mins. 600W *(3 mins. 700W; 5 mins. 500W)*, stirring once or twice.

4   Sprinkle over the flour, ≋ FULL for 1 min. 600W *(30 secs. 700W; 1 min. 500W)*, then pour over the milk and ≋ FULL for 2 mins. *(1½ mins. 700W; 2½ mins. 500W)*, stirring once or twice.

5   Mix in the cooked millet and season the mixture well with salt and pepper.

6   To make the crust, mix the self-raising flour with the salt and rub in the fat. Add the milk gradually and mix to a soft dough.

7   Use two-thirds of the dough, rolled out quite thinly, to line a 900ml (1½ pint) basin. Spoon in the filling, then cover with the remaining dough. Cover with greaseproof paper and a plate, then ≋ FULL for 9 mins. 600W *(7½ mins. 700W; 11 mins. 500W)*, giving the basin a quarter turn every 2 mins. Leave to stand for 2-3 mins. Serve with a mushroom or onion sauce.

★ **Preparation:**
25 minutes

≋ **Cooking time:**
31 minutes

⊘ **Power setting:**
FULL

◎ **Serves 4**

Illustrated opposite

Walnut and bulgar pilaff

INGREDIENTS

100g (4 oz) chopped walnuts
15ml (1 tbsp) olive oil
3 spring onions, diced
1 clove garlic, crushed
100g (4 oz) bulgar wheat
2 medium green peppers, deseeded and diced
400g (14 oz) can tomatoes
30ml (2 tbsp) chopped fresh mint
large pinch ground cinnamon
large pinch ground cloves
300ml (½ pint) boiling water
salt and black pepper
Garnish
6 spring onions

Bulgar wheat is ideal for microwaved dishes, either in a simple pilaff or as the basis for a stuffing in vegetables such as peppers or tomatoes.

1   Spread out the walnuts on a small plate and ≋ FULL for 3 mins. 600W *(2½ mins. 700W; 3½ mins. 500W)*. Set aside.

2   Put the oil in a medium dish and ≋ FULL for 1 min. 600W *(30 secs. 700W; 1 min. 500W)*. Add the spring onions and garlic and ≋ FULL for 30 secs.

3   Add the remaining ingredients, except the nuts and seasoning, cover and ≋ FULL for 6 mins. 600W *(5 mins. 700W; 7½ mins. 500W)*, stirring once.

4   Season well with salt and pepper, then quickly stir in the chopped walnuts.

5   Garnish with spring onions and serve with a green salad.

★ **Preparation:**
15 minutes

≋ **Cooking time:**
10½ minutes

⊘ **Power setting:**
FULL

◎ **Serves 4**

Illustrated opposite

Top: **Polenta with tomato sauce** *(see p. 43)*; Centre: **Millet and mushroom bake** *(see above)*; Bottom: **Walnut and bulgar pilaff** *(see above)*

Spicy layered mango pilaff

INGREDIENTS

15ml (1 tbsp) sunflower oil
3 spring onions, finely chopped
1-2 cloves garlic, crushed
5ml (1 tsp) garam masala
5ml (1 tsp) cumin seeds
2.5ml (½ tsp) turmeric
50g (2 oz) pine kernels
175g (6 oz) long-grain brown rice
750ml (1¼ pints) boiling water
1 mango, peeled and diced
juice of ½ lemon

For the filling

15ml (1 tbsp) sunflower oil
225g (8 oz) mushrooms, diced
1 clove garlic, chopped
100g (4 oz) French beans, diced
15ml (1 tbsp) shoyu

The filling for this pilaff consists of a simple mixture of fresh vegetables which can be varied according to availability.

1 Put the oil in a medium dish and ≋ FULL for 1 min. 600W *(30 secs. 700W; 1 min. 500W)*. Stir in the onion and garlic and ≋ FULL for 30 secs.

2 Mix the spices with a little water. Add to the onions with the pine kernels and ≋ FULL for 30 secs.

3 Add the rice and boiling water. Cover and ≋ FULL for about 18 mins. *(all powers)*, stirring 2-3 times. Leave to stand for 5 mins. Then add the mango and the lemon juice. Season well.

4 For the filling, put the oil in a medium dish and ≋ FULL for 1 min. 600W *(30 secs. 700W; 1 min. 500W)*. Stir in the diced mushrooms and garlic, cover and ≋ FULL for 3 mins. 600W *(2½ mins. 700W; 3½ mins. 500W)*.

5 Add the beans, shoyu and 15ml (1 tbsp) water. Re-cover and ≋ FULL for 4 mins. 600W *(3 mins. 700W; 5 mins. 500W)*. Season well.

6 Put half the rice into a large dish and cover with the mushroom and bean mixture. Spoon over the remaining rice, cover and ≋ FULL for 3 mins. 600W *(2½ mins. 700W; 3½ mins. 500W)*.

★ **Preparation:** 25 minutes

≋ **Cooking time:** 31 minutes

∅ **Power setting:** FULL

❋ **Freezes well**

◎ **Serves 4**

≋ The cooking time for rice will vary according to the age and variety of the grain. If it's not quite tender at the end of the time recommended here, cook for a little longer, adding a little more boiling water if necessary.

Illustrated opposite

Leek and cauliflower cobbler

INGREDIENTS

10ml (2 tsp) sunflower oil
1 medium leek, diced
450g (1 lb) cauliflower, divided into florets

For the sauce

15g (½ oz) margarine
15ml (1 tbsp) wholewheat flour
300ml (½ pint) skimmed milk
1 bay leaf
2.5ml (½ tsp) grated nutmeg
5ml (1 tsp) mustard powder

For the topping

75g (3 oz) wholewheat flour
75g (3 oz) cornmeal
7.5ml (1½ tsp) baking powder
2.5ml (½ tsp) salt
5ml (1 tsp) caraway seeds
2.5ml (½ tsp) mustard powder
1 egg
150ml (¼ pint) milk
15ml (1 tbsp) olive oil
50g (2 oz) Cheddar cheese, grated

In this dish the lightly cooked vegetables retain a good crisp texture, the sauce is easy to prepare, and the scone topping provides a tasty and wholesome finish.

1 Put the oil in a medium dish and ≋ FULL for 1 min. 600W *(30 secs. 700W; 1 min. 500W)*. Add the leek and cauliflower, cover and ≋ FULL for 4 mins. 600W *(3 mins. 700W; 5 mins. 500W)*. Leave to stand.

2 For the sauce, put the margarine in a 600ml (1 pint) jug and ≋ FULL for 1 min. 600W *(30 secs. 700W; 1 min 500W)*. Add the flour and ≋ FULL for 30 secs. Pour in the milk, stirring well. Add the bay leaf and spices, then ≋ FULL for 2 mins. 600W *(1½ mins. 700W; 2½ mins. 500W)*, stirring every 30 secs. Season well, then mix into the vegetables.

3 For the topping, mix the wholewheat flour, cornmeal, baking powder, salt and spices together.

4 In a separate jug, beat the egg thoroughly, then add the milk and olive oil. Pour the mixture over the dry ingredients and mix to a stiff dough. Add the cheese. Roll out the dough and cut into 2.5cm (1 in) rounds about 1cm (½ in) deep.

5 Put the vegetables and sauce in a medium dish and cover with the scone rounds. ≋ FULL for 5 mins. 600W *(4 mins. 700W; 6 mins. 500W)*, then brown under a preheated conventional grill.

★ **Preparation:** 30 minutes

≋ **Cooking time:** 13½ minutes

∅ **Power setting:** FULL

◎ **Serves 4**

◎ If wished, top with a little more grated cheese before browning under a conventional grill.

Illustrated opposite

Top: **Spicy layered mango pilaff** *(see above)*; Bottom: **Leek and cauliflower cobbler** *(see above)*

Stuffed cabbage leaves

INGREDIENTS

100g (4 oz) pot barley
600ml (1 pint) boiling water
75g (3 oz) sunflower seeds
1 medium onion, finely chopped
175g (6 oz) button mushrooms, diced
100g (4 oz) cabbage, shredded
1 apple, grated
5ml (1 tsp) caraway seeds
100g (4 oz) carrots, grated
15ml (1 tbsp) shoyu
salt and black pepper
8-12 cabbage leaves

For the sauce

225g (8 oz) cooked carrots
30ml (2 tbsp) orange juice
60ml (4 tbsp) yogurt
2.5ml (½ tsp) grated nutmeg
salt and black pepper

Barley is an underrated grain all too often confined to soups. It has a delicate flavour and is ideal as a vegetable filling.

1   Put the barley in a deep dish and pour over the boiling water. Leave to soak for 1 hour. Cover and ≋ FULL for 20 mins. *(all powers)*, stirring 2-3 times. Stand for 5 mins. then drain.

2   Spread out the sunflower seeds on a small plate and ≋ FULL for 2 mins. 600W *(1½ mins. 700W; 2½ mins. 500W).*

3   Put the oil in a medium dish and ≋ FULL for 1 min. 600W *(30 secs. 700W; 1 min. 500W).* Add the onion and ≋ FULL for 2 mins. 600W *(1½ mins. 700W; 2½ mins. 500W).* Stir in the mushrooms, shredded cabbage, apple and caraway. Cover and ≋ FULL for 4 mins. 600W *(3 mins. 700W; 5 mins. 500W).*

4   Mix the cooked vegetables and barley with the raw carrot, sunflower seeds and shoyu. Season well with salt and pepper.

5   To soften the cabbage leaves, place in a large dish with 30ml (2 tbsp) water. Cover and ≋ FULL for 2 mins. 600W *(1½ mins. 700W; 2½ mins. 500W).* Spoon 15-30ml (1-2 tbsp) filling on to each cabbage leaf, then roll up to make neat parcels. Arrange these in a shallow dish, cover and ≋ FULL for 3 mins. 600W *(2½ mins. 700W; 3½ mins. 500W)* or until heated through.

6   To make the sauce, purée the cooked carrots with the orange juice and yogurt, and season well. ≋ FULL for 1½ mins. 600W *(1 min. 700W; 2 mins. 500W)* then serve.

 Preparation: 25 minutes

Cooking time: 44 minutes

Power setting: FULL

Serves 4

Choose dark leaves such as the outer leaves of a January King or Savoy for this recipe or the end result will look very pale.

Illustrated below

Stuffed tomatoes

INGREDIENTS

4 large beef tomatoes
50g (2 oz) peanuts
15ml (1 tbsp) sesame seeds
5ml (1 tsp) cumin seeds
5ml (1 tsp) coriander seeds
50-75g (2-3 oz) wholewheat breadcrumbs
50g (2 oz) black olives, stoned and chopped
2 sticks celery, diced
4 spring onions, diced
15ml (1 tbsp) tomato purée
10ml (2 tsp) miso, dissolved in a little stock
salt and black pepper

The spicy flavour of the roasted nut and seed filling complements the sweet, moist tomatoes perfectly

1 Slice a lid from the base of each tomato, then scoop out the flesh and chop well.

2 Mix the peanuts, sesame seeds and spices together, spread out on a small plate and ≋ FULL for 3 mins. 600W *(2½ mins. 700W; 3½ mins. 500W)*, shaking the plate once or twice. Grind quite finely.

3 Mix the ground nuts and seeds with about half of the tomato flesh and the remaining ingredients, seasoning well with salt and pepper. Fill the tomatoes with the mixture and cover each one with its lid.

4 Arrange the tomatoes in a large dish, cover and ≋ FULL for 7 mins. 600W *(6 mins. 700W; 8½ mins. 500W)*, rearranging once or twice during cooking.

5 Serve hot with a tomato sauce or sharp yogurt dressing.

 Preparation: 25 minutes

≋ **Cooking time:** 10 minutes

⊘ **Power setting:** FULL

◎ **Serves 4**

≋ Be careful not to overcook the tomato shells or they will collapse; keep a close watch during the last 2-3 mins. of cooking.

Illustrated below

Far left and right: **Stuffed cabbage leaves** *(see above, left)*; Centre: **Stuffed tomatoes** *(see above)*

Hazelnut roast

INGREDIENTS

100g (4 oz) short-grain brown rice
450ml (¾ pint) boiling water
100g (4 oz) hazelnuts
15ml (1 tbsp) sunflower oil
1 medium onion, finely chopped
2 cloves garlic, crushed
5ml (1 tsp) celery seeds
100g (4 oz) carrots, diced
15ml (1 tbsp) wholewheat flour
150ml (¼ pint) red wine
30ml (2 tbsp) tomato purée
salt and black pepper

Using grains instead of breadcrumbs in a nut roast makes the mixture chewy in texture, but lighter and more moist.

1   Put the rice in a deep dish and pour over the boiling water. Cover and ≋ FULL for 18 mins. *(all powers)*, stirring 2-3 times. Leave to stand for 5 mins.

2   Spread out the hazelnuts on a small plate and ≋ FULL for 4 mins. 600W *(3 mins. 700W; 5 mins. 500W)*, shaking the plate once or twice. Cool and grind.

3   Put the oil in a medium dish and ≋ FULL for 1 min. 600W *(30 secs. 700W; 1 min. 500W)*. Stir in the onion, then ≋ FULL for 1 min. 600W *(30 secs. 700W; 1 min. 500W)*.

4   Add the garlic, celery seeds and carrots and ≋ FULL for 4 mins. 600W *(3 mins. 700W; 5 mins. 500W)*.

5   Sprinkle over the flour and ≋ FULL for 30 secs.

6   Stir in the wine and tomato purée, cover and ≋ FULL for 2 mins. 600W *(1½ mins. 700W; 2½ mins. 500W)*.

7   Mix the ground nuts and the rice into the sauce and season well with salt and pepper.

8   Line a 450g (1 lb) loaf dish with greaseproof paper and spoon in the mixture. Cover with more paper and stand the dish on an upturned plate or saucer in the microwave. ≋ FULL for 10-12 mins. 600W *(8½-10 mins. 700W; 12½-15 mins. 500W)*, giving the dish a quarter turn every 3 mins. Leave to stand for 4 mins. before turning out and serving.

Preparation:
20 minutes

Cooking time:
40½ minutes

Power setting:
FULL

Serves 4

Nut roasts are best when slightly undercooked and then left to stand to finish. If overcooked, the outsides become dry and hard.

Illustrated opposite

Creamy almond bake

INGREDIENTS

175g (6 oz) blanched almonds
15ml (1 tbsp) sunflower oil
1 medium onion, finely chopped
2 sticks celery, diced
175g (6 oz) button mushrooms, diced
100g (4 oz) white cabbage, shredded
15ml (1 tbsp) shoyu
10ml (2 tsp) horseradish
5ml (1 tsp) ready-made mustard
1 egg, beaten
50g (2 oz) oat flakes
salt and black pepper

Nut roast mixtures cook quickly and well in the microwave, but it is important that the mixture is quite moist and well flavoured.

1   Spread out the almonds on a small plate and ≋ FULL for 3-4 mins. 600W *(2½-3 mins. 700W; 3½-5 mins. 500W)* until toasted, shaking the dish several times. Grind finely.

2   Put the oil in a medium dish and ≋ FULL for 1 min. 600W *(30 secs. 700W; 1 min. 500W)*. Stir in the onion and ≋ FULL for 2 mins. 600W *(1½ mins. 700W; 2½ mins. 500W)*.

3   Add the celery, mushrooms, cabbage, shoyu, horseradish and mustard. Cover and ≋ FULL for 6 mins. 600W *(5 mins. 700W; 7½ mins. 500W)*, stirring once or twice.

4   Liquidize until smooth, then stir in the toasted nuts, beaten egg and oat flakes. Season to taste.

5   Line a 450g (1 lb) loaf dish with greaseproof paper and spoon in the mixture. Cover with more paper and stand the dish on an upturned plate or saucer in the microwave. ≋ FULL for 10 mins. 600W *(8½ mins. 700W; 12½ mins. 500W)*, giving the dish a quarter turn every 2½ mins. Leave to stand for 5 mins. before turning out and serving with a contrasting sauce.

Preparation:
25 minutes

Cooking time:
22 minutes

Power setting:
FULL

Serves 3-4

For a browned effect, lightly grill the bake once it has been turned out of the loaf dish.

Illustrated opposite

Top: **Saffron rice with mangetout** *(see p. 52)*; Centre: **Hazelnut roast** *(see above)*; Bottom: **Creamy almond bake** *(see above)*

Saffron rice with mangetout

INGREDIENTS

15ml (1 tbsp) sesame oil
1 medium onion, chopped
1 clove garlic, crushed
1cm (½ in) piece fresh root ginger, grated
5ml (1 tsp) ground coriander
200g (7 oz) can tomatoes, drained and mashed
5ml (1 tsp) ground saffron
175g (6 oz) brown rice
750ml (1¼ pints) boiling water
225g (8 oz) mangetout
1 medium green pepper, deseeded and diced
75g (3 oz) mung bean sprouts
½ cucumber, diced
For the sauce
juice of 1 orange
juice of ½ lemon
15ml (1 tbsp) shoyu
15ml (1 tbsp) sherry
5ml (1 tsp) arrowroot

Grain dishes topped with mixtures of lightly cooked vegetables are really easy in the microwave. Here, saffron, ginger and coriander add an exotic flavour to the rice while the vegetables give a fresh, crisp texture.

1   Put the oil in a medium dish and ≋ FULL for 1 min. 600W *(30 secs. 700W; 1 min. 500W)*. Stir in the onion and garlic and ≋ FULL for 30 secs. Stir well.

2   Add the ginger, coriander, tomatoes, saffron and rice. Pour over the boiling water, cover and ≋ FULL for 18 mins. *(all powers)*, stirring 2-3 times.

3   Add the vegetables. re-cover and ≋ FULL for 4 mins. 600W *(3 mins. 700W; 5 mins. 500W)*. Leave to stand for 4 mins.

4   For the sauce, mix the fruit juices, shoyu and sherry together in a small jug, then ≋ FULL for 2 mins. 600W *(1½ mins. 700W; 2½ mins. 500W)*.

5   Dissolve the arrowroot in a little water, then stir into the sauce. ≋ FULL for 2 mins. 600W *(1½ mins. 700W; 2½ mins. 500W)*, stirring twice.

6   Pour the sauce over the rice and vegetables and serve.

 Preparation: 20 minutes

Cooking time: 27½ minutes

Power setting: FULL

Serves 4

Illustrated on p. 50

Lentil and vegetable loaf

INGREDIENTS

50g (2 oz) continental or brown lentils
600ml (1 pint) boiling water
1 potato, weighing about 175g (6 oz)
15ml (1 tbsp) sunflower oil
100g (4 oz) leeks, trimmed and diced
1 medium carrot, diced
100g (4 oz) mushrooms, chopped
10ml (2 tsp) chopped fresh sage
10ml (2 tsp) miso
50ml (2 fl oz) bean stock or dark vegetable stock
15ml (1 tbsp) tomato purée
50g (2 oz) porridge oats
25g (1 oz) breadcrumbs
15g (½ oz) sunflower margarine
15g (½ oz) wholewheat flour
15ml (1 tbsp) shoyu
5ml (1 tsp) yeast extract
black pepper

This hearty savoury loaf is full of rich flavours and moist vegetables. It is a good dish for a family supper, served with baked potatoes and green vegetables.

1   Put the lentils in a deep dish and pour over the boiling water. Cover and ≋ FULL for 12 mins. *(all powers)*, stirring 2-3 times. Leave to stand for 5 mins. then drain.

2   Pierce the potato and wrap in absorbent paper. ≋ FULL for 6 mins. 600W *(5 mins. 700W; 7½ mins. 500W)*, turning over halfway through. Leave to cool slightly, then dice.

3   Put the oil in a medium dish and ≋ FULL for 1 min. 600W *(30 secs. 700W; 1 min. 500W)*. Stir in the leeks and ≋ FULL for 3 mins. 600W *(2½ mins. 700W; 3½ mins. 500W)*.

4   Add the carrot, mushrooms, potato, sage and the miso dissolved in a little of the stock. Cover and ≋ FULL for 5 mins. *(4 mins. 700W; 6 mins. 500W)*, stirring once or twice. Stir in the tomato purée, oats, breadcrumbs and lentils.

5   Put the margarine in a separate dish and ≋ FULL for 30 secs. Stir in the flour and ≋ FULL for 30 secs. Add the remaining bean stock, shoyu and yeast extract. ≋ FULL for 1-1½ mins. stirring once.

6   Stir the sauce into the lentil and vegetable mixture. Season to taste. Spoon into 450g (1 lb) loaf dish and ≋ FULL for 10 mins. 600W *(8½ mins. 700W; 12½ mins. 500W)*. Leave to stand for 5 mins. before turning out and serving.

 Preparation: 20 minutes

Cooking time: 39 minutes

Power setting: FULL

Good reheated

Freezes well

Serves 4

 Savoury loaves also cook well in savarin moulds as the microwaves can penetrate from all sides.

Illustrated opposite

Top: **Borlotti bean casserole** *(see p. 54)*; Bottom right: **Lentil and vegetable loaf** *(see above)*; Bottom left: **Aubergine layer** *(see p. 54)*

Borlotti bean casserole

INGREDIENTS

225g (8 oz) borlotti or pinto beans, soaked overnight
1.2 litre (2 pints) boiling water
15ml (1 tbsp) olive oil
1 onion, finely chopped
1 clove garlic, crushed
225g (8 oz) courgettes, diced
1 medium green pepper, deseeded and diced
400g (14 oz) can tomatoes, mashed
1 bay leaf
15ml (1 tbsp) tomato purée
salt and black pepper
For the pesto
25g (1 oz) pine kernels
15g (½ oz) Parmesan cheese, grated
60ml (4 tbsp) chopped fresh basil
15ml (1 tbsp) olive oil
1-2 cloves garlic
salt and black pepper

Pesto sauce adds a wonderful flavour to any savoury dish. It is particularly good in microwaved stews where the quick cooking means the flavours of the ingredients don't have time to blend.

1 For the pesto, grind the pine kernels using a pestle and mortar, then work in the other ingredients to form a smooth paste. Set aside.

2 Drain the beans, put in a deep dish and pour over the boiling water. Cover and ≋ FULL for 22 mins. *(all powers)*, stirring 2-3 times and adding more boiling water if necessary. Leave to stand for 10 mins. then drain.

3 Put the oil in a medium dish and ≋ FULL for 1 min. 600W *(30 secs. 700W; 1 min. 500W)*. Stir in the onion and garlic and ≋ FULL for 2 mins. 600W *(1½ mins. 700W; 2½ mins. 500W)*.

4 Add the courgettes, pepper and cooked beans, stir well and ≋ FULL for 5 mins. 600W *(4 mins. 700W; 6 mins. 500W)*, stirring once or twice.

5 Add the tomatoes, bay leaf and purée. Cover and ≋ FULL for 5 mins. 600W *(4 mins. 700W; 6 mins. 500W)*.

6 Add the pesto sauce and ≋ FULL for 5 mins. 600W *(4 mins. 700W; 6 mins. 500W)*. Leave to stand for 5 mins. then season to taste. Serve hot with rice, noodles, pasta or jacket potatoes.

★ **Preparation:** 20 minutes, plus overnight soaking

≋ **Cooking time:** 40 minutes

⊘ **Power setting:** FULL

≈ **Good reheated**

◎ **Serves 4**

Illustrated on p. 53

Aubergine layer

INGREDIENTS

1 large aubergine, weighing about 350g (12 oz)
1 large potato, weighing about 225g (8 oz)
15ml (1 tbsp) olive oil
1 medium onion, finely chopped
1-2 cloves garlic, crushed
3 sticks celery, diced
1 medium green pepper, deseeded and diced
1 medium red pepper, deseeded and diced
400g (14 oz) can tomatoes
30ml (2 tbsp) chopped fresh basil
100g (4 oz) hard Greek cheese (Haloumi), cubed
salt and black pepper

This deliciously rich dish is much easier to prepare in the microwave. Whole aubergines and potatoes take only a few minutes to bake and the dish is completed with a quick sauce.

1 Trim the aubergine and pierce the skin. Wrap in absorbent paper and ≋ FULL for 3 mins. 600W *(2½ mins. 700W; 3½ mins. 500W)* until tender but still firm, turning over halfway through. Leave to stand for 4 mins. then slice thinly.

2 Pierce the potato and wrap in absorbent paper. ≋ FULL for 4 mins. 600W *(3 mins. 700W; 5 mins. 500W)*, turning over halfway through. Leave to stand for 5 mins. then slice thinly.

3 Put the oil in a medium dish and ≋ FULL for 1 min. 600W *(30 secs. 700W; 1 min. 500W)*. Stir in the onion and ≋ FULL for 2 mins. 600W *(1½ mins. 700W; 2½ mins. 500W)*.

4 Add the garlic, celery and peppers. Stir well, cover and ≋ FULL for 4 mins. 600W *(3 mins. 700W; 5 mins. 500W)*.

5 Add the tomatoes and basil. Cover and ≋ FULL for 5 mins. 600W *(4 mins. 700W; 6 mins. 500W)*, stirring once. Season well with salt and pepper.

6 Put a layer of sauce in the base of a deep, medium-sized dish and cover with layers of sliced potato, aubergine and cubes of cheese. Continue layering, finishing with sauce then cheese.

7 ≋ MEDIUM-HIGH for 8 mins. *(6 mins. 700W; ≋ FULL for 6-7 mins. 500W)* until the cheese has just melted, giving the dish a quarter turn every 2 mins. Leave to stand for 4 mins.

★ **Preparation:** 25 minutes

≋ **Cooking time:** 27 minutes

⊘ **Power settings:** FULL and MEDIUM-HIGH

≈ **Good reheated**

❋ **Freezes well**

◎ **Serves 4**

Illustrated on p. 53

Mushroom stroganov

INGREDIENTS

15ml (1 tbsp) sunflower oil
2 small onions, finely chopped
1 clove garlic, crushed
350g (12 oz) button mushrooms, quartered
300g (10 oz) green beans, sliced
1 medium red pepper, deseeded and diced
10ml (2 tsp) paprika
10ml (2 tsp) dill weed
5ml (1 tsp) chopped fresh thyme
15ml (1 tbsp) shoyu
100ml (4 fl oz) single cream
100ml (4 fl oz) yogurt
5ml (1 tsp) cornflour
4-6 drops Tabasco sauce
salt and black pepper

A delicious and simple dish with a surprising contrast of textures: crisp vegetables in a rich, creamy sauce.

1   Put the oil in a medium dish and ≋ FULL for 1 min. 600W *(30 secs. 700W; 1 min. 500W)*. Stir in the chopped onion and the garlic and ≋ FULL for 2 mins. 600W *(1½ mins. 700W; 2½ mins. 500W)*.

2   Add the vegetables, paprika, herbs and shoyu. Cover and ≋ FULL for 8 mins. 600W *(6½ mins. 700W; 10 mins. 500W)*, stirring once or twice.

3   Mix the cream, yogurt and cornflour together, then stir into the vegetables. Add the Tabasco sauce and season well with salt and pepper. ≋ MEDIUM-HIGH for 2 mins. 600W *(1½ mins. 700W; ≋ FULL for 1½ mins. 500W)* until just heated through, stirring every minute. Serve with brown rice, wholewheat pasta or buckwheat noodles.

★ **Preparation:**
20 minutes

≋ **Cooking time:**
13 minutes

⌀ **Power settings:**
FULL and MEDIUM-HIGH

≋ **Good reheated**

❇ **Freezes well**

◎ **Serves 4**

★ For a low fat version, use all yogurt in the sauce instead of cream.

Illustrated on p. 56

Moussaka

INGREDIENTS

1 aubergine, weighing about 225g (8 oz)
1 large potato, weighing about 350g (12 oz)
15ml (1 tbsp) olive oil
1 medium onion, finely chopped
1 clove garlic, crushed
2 sticks celery, diced
400g (14 oz) can tomatoes
50g (2 oz) bulgar wheat
1 bay leaf
5ml (1 tsp) chopped fresh thyme
5ml (1 tsp) dried oregano
2.5ml (½ tsp) ground cinnamon
15ml (1 tbsp) shoyu
salt and black pepper
300ml (½ pint) yogurt
2 eggs, beaten
15-30ml (1-2 tbsp) lemon juice

This version of moussaka is quite light and fragrant as it is layered with a lemon-flavoured yogurt sauce. The texture and substance are provided by the bulgar wheat.

1   Trim the aubergine, then pierce the skin. Wrap in absorbent paper and ≋ FULL for 3 mins. 600W *(2½ mins. 700W; 3½ mins. 500W)* until tender but still firm, turning over halfway through. Leave to cool, then cube.

2   Pierce the potato and wrap in absorbent paper. ≋ FULL for 6 mins. 600W *(5 mins. 700W; 7½ mins. 500W)*, turning over halfway through. Leave to cool slightly, then slice.

3   Put the oil in a medium dish and ≋ FULL for 1 min. 600W *(30 secs. 700W; 1 min. 500W)*. Stir in the chopped onion and the garlic and ≋ FULL for 2 mins. 600W *(1½ mins. 700W; 2½ mins. 500W)*.

4   Add the aubergine and celery and ≋ FULL for 2 mins. 600W *(1½ mins. 700W; 2½ mins. 500W)*.

5   Stir in the tomatoes, bulgar wheat, herbs, cinnamon and shoyu. Cover and ≋ FULL for 7 mins. 600W *(6 mins. 700W; 8½ mins. 500W)*, stirring once or twice. Discard the bay leaf, then season to taste with salt and pepper.

6   In a separate bowl, beat the yogurt, eggs and lemon juice together with a fork or balloon whisk. Season to taste.

7   Put a layer of the aubergine mixture in a medium dish, then cover with layers of potato and yogurt sauce. Continue layering, finishing with yogurt sauce.

8   ≋ MEDIUM-HIGH for 10 mins. 600W *(8½ mins. 700W; ≋ FULL for 8½ mins. 500W)*, giving the dish a half turn halfway through. Leave to stand for 3-4 mins. before serving.

★ **Preparation:**
25 minutes

≋ **Cooking time:**
31 minutes

⌀ **Power setting:**
FULL

≋ **Good reheated**

❇ **Freezes well**

◎ **Serves 4**

≋ Finish under a conventional grill if you want to brown the topping.

Illustrated on p. 56

Lasagne with lentils

Always a popular main course, the microwave takes a lot of the work and washing up out of this recipe. Make sure that both sauces are well flavoured so the dish has a well-rounded taste.

INGREDIENTS

175g (6 oz) continental lentils
900ml (1½ pint) boiling water
30ml (2 tbsp) sunflower oil
1 medium onion, finely chopped
2 cloves garlic, crushed
1 aubergine, weighing about 225g (8 oz), chopped
100g (4 oz) carrots, diced
400g (14 oz) can tomatoes
30ml (2 tbsp) tomato purée
30ml (2 tbsp) shoyu
5ml (1 tsp) chopped fresh thyme
5ml (1 tsp) chopped fresh marjoram
salt and black pepper
450ml (¾ pint) skimmed milk
½ medium onion
1 bay leaf
6 peppercorns
sprig of parsley
sprig of thyme
25g (1 oz) sunflower margarine
25g (1 oz) wholewheat flour
8-10 pieces lasagne (pre-cooked wholewheat variety)
75g (3 oz) Cheddar cheese, grated

1 Put the lentils in a deep bowl and pour over the boiling water. Cover and ≋ FULL for 12-15 mins. *(all powers)*, stirring 2-3 times. Leave to stand for 5 mins. then drain.

2 Put the oil in a medium dish and ≋ FULL for 1 min. 600W *(30 secs. 700W; 1 min. 500W)*. Stir in the chopped onion and the garlic, then ≋ FULL for 2 mins. 600W *(1½ mins. 700W; 2½ mins. 500W)*.

3 Add the aubergine and carrots, cover and ≋ FULL for 5 mins. 600W *(4 mins. 700W; 6 mins. 500W)*, stirring once.

4 Add the tomatoes, purée, shoyu, herbs and lentils. Re-cover and ≋ FULL for 5 mins. 600W *(4 mins. 700W; 6 mins. 500W)*, stirring once. Season well.

5 Put the milk, onion, bay leaf, peppercorns and herbs in a jug and ≋ FULL for 3½ mins. 600W *(2½ mins. 700W; 4 mins. 500W)*. Leave to stand for 5 mins. then strain.

6 Put the margarine in a medium dish and ≋ FULL for 30 secs. Stir in the flour and ≋ FULL for 30 secs. then pour in the infused milk, stirring well. ≋ FULL for 2-3 mins. 600W *(1½-2 mins. 700W; 2½-3½ mins. 500W)*, stirring every minute.

7 In a medium dish, layer pieces of lasagne with the lentil and tomato sauce and the white sauce, finishing with white sauce. Cover with grated cheese and ≋ FULL for 6 mins. 600W *(5 mins. 700W; 7½ mins. 500W)*, giving the dish a quarter turn every 2 mins. Brown under a preheated conventional grill.

★ **Preparation:** 35 minutes

≋ **Cooking time:** 35 minutes

⊘ **Power setting:** FULL

≈ **Good reheated**

❋ **Freezes well**

◎ **Serves 4**

★ Use the type of lasagne that does not require pre-cooking; If unavailable put ordinary lasagne in a large bowl of boiling water and ≋ FULL for 8-10 mins. *(all powers)*. Leave to stand for 5-10 mins. then drain.

Illustrated opposite

Piperade

This classic French dish is a moist mixture of vegetables bound together with scrambled egg. As well as being a breakfast or supper dish, it can also be used as a filling for baked potatoes. The tip below explains how to make plain scrambled egg.

INGREDIENTS

15ml (1 tbsp) olive oil
1 large onion, finely chopped
1-2 cloves garlic, crushed
1 medium red pepper, deseeded and diced
1 medium green pepper, deseeded and diced
5ml (1 tsp) fines herbes or 15ml (1 tbsp) mixed chopped fresh chives and tarragon
15ml (1 tbsp) finely chopped fresh parsley
3 eggs, beaten
30-45ml (2-3 tbsp) milk
salt and black pepper

1 Put the oil in a medium dish and ≋ FULL for 1 min. 600W *(30 secs. 700W; 1 min. 500W)*. Stir in the chopped onion and the garlic and ≋ FULL for 2 mins. 600W *(1½ mins. 700W; 2½ mins. 500W)*.

2 Add the diced red and green peppers, stir well, and ≋ FULL for 3 mins. 600W *(2½ mins. 700W; 3½ mins. 500W)*, stirring once or twice.

3 Mix in the herbs, beaten eggs and milk. ≋ FULL for 2½-3 mins. 600W *(2-2½ mins. 700W; 3-3½ mins. 500W)*, stirring once or twice. Season well and serve immediately.

★ **Preparation:** 15 minutes

≋ **Cooking time:** 8½ minutes

⊘ **Power setting:** FULL

◎ **Serves 2**

★ To make scrambled egg for one, put 15g (½ oz) butter in a small dish and ≋ FULL for 30 secs. Beat in 2 eggs and 30ml (2 tbsp) milk. ≋ FULL for 1 min. Beat well, then ≋ FULL for a further 30 secs. Season to taste with salt and pepper and serve immediately.

Illustrated on p. 59

Clockwise from the top: **Moussaka** *(see p. 55)*; **Mushroom stroganoff** *(see p. 55)*; **Lasagne with lentils** *(see above)*

Broccoli and leek croustade

INGREDIENTS

100g (4 oz) ground almonds
100g (4 oz) breadcrumbs
1 clove garlic, crushed
30ml (2 tbsp) olive oil
50g (2 oz) Cheddar cheese, grated
5ml (1 tsp) chopped fresh rosemary
For the topping
25g (1 oz) sunflower margarine or butter
225g (8 oz) broccoli, chopped
225g (8 oz) leeks, diced
25g (1 oz) wholewheat flour
300ml (½ pint) skimmed milk
salt and black pepper
50g (2 oz) Cheddar cheese, grated

The croustade base cooks very well in the microwave, and it doesn't matter that it is pale as it is hidden under the colourful vegetable topping.

1   Mix the almonds, breadcrumbs and garlic together. Work in the oil, then mix in the cheese and rosemary.

2   Press the mixture into a 20cm (8 in) round dish and ≋ FULL for 4 mins. 600W *(3 mins. 700W; 5 mins. 500W),* giving the dish a quarter turn every minute.

3   To make the topping, put the margarine in a medium dish and ≋ FULL for 30 secs. Stir in the vegetables, cover and ≋ FULL for 3 mins. 600W *(2½ mins. 700W; 3½ mins. 500W).* Sprinkle over the flour and ≋ FULL for 30 secs.

4   Pour over the milk, stir well, and ≋ FULL for 2-3 mins. 600W *(1½-2½ mins. 700W; 2½-3½ mins. 500W),* stirring every minute until boiling point is reached. Season to taste.

5   Pour the topping over the base and sprinkle over the grated cheese. ≋ FULL for 4 mins. 600W *(3 mins. 700W; 5 mins. 500W).* Brown under a preheated grill before serving.

★ **Preparation:** 20 minutes

≋ **Cooking time:** 14 minutes

⊘ **Power setting:** FULL

≋ **Good reheated**

◎ **Serves 4**

Illustrated opposite

Cottage pie with leeks and lentils

INGREDIENTS

100g (4 oz) brown lentils
900ml (1½ pints) boiling water
2 potatoes, weighing about 225g (8 oz) each
15ml (1 tbsp) shoyu
30ml (2 tbsp) chopped fresh parsley
30ml (2 tbsp) sunflower oil
350g (12 oz) leeks, diced
225g (8 oz) carrots, diced
1 small cauliflower, divided into florets
For the mushroom sauce
15ml (1 tbsp) sunflower oil
175g (6 oz) mushrooms, diced
5ml (1 tsp) paprika
5 ml (1 tsp) chopped fresh sage
15ml (1 tbsp) shoyu
salt and black pepper

Brown lentils are a useful ingredient in both a vegetarian and a microwave diet. They cook quickly, have a good texture and absorb other flavours well.

1   Put the lentils in a deep dish, pour over the boiling water, cover and ≋ FULL for 12 mins. *(all powers),* stirring 2-3 times. Leave to stand for 5 mins. then drain, reserving the stock.

2   Pierce the potatoes and wrap in absorbent paper. ≋ FULL for 8 mins. 600W *(6½ mins. 700W; 10 mins. 500W),* turning over and rearranging halfway through. Leave to cool, then mash the flesh. Stir in the shoyu, parsley and 15ml (1 tbsp) oil.

3   Put the remaining 15ml (1 tbsp) oil in a medium dish and ≋ FULL for 1 min. 600W *(30 secs. 700W; 1 min. 500W).* Stir in the leeks, carrots and cauliflower and ≋ FULL for 1 min. Add 90ml (6 tbsp) water, cover and ≋ FULL for 6 mins. 600W *(5 mins. 700W; 7½ mins. 500W),* stirring once. Stir in the lentils.

4   For the sauce, put the oil in a separate medium dish and ≋ FULL for 1 min. 600W *(30 secs. 700W; 1 min. 500W).* Stir in the mushrooms and ≋ FULL for 4 mins. 600W *(3 mins. 700W; 5 mins. 500W),* stirring once or twice.

5   Liquidize until smooth, adding a little lentil stock. Stir in to the vegetables and mix in the paprika, sage and shoyu. Season well with salt and pepper.

6   Spoon the vegetables into a dish, top with the mashed potato and ≋ MEDIUM-HIGH for 5-6 mins. 600W *(4-5 mins. 700W; ≋ FULL for 4-5 mins. 500W),* giving the dish a half turn halfway through. Leave to stand for 3 mins. Brown under a preheated conventional grill if you prefer a crisped topping.

★ **Preparation:** 25 minutes

≋ **Cooking time:** 38 minutes

⊘ **Power settings:** FULL and MEDIUM-HIGH

≋ **Good reheated**

✳ **Freezes well**

◎ **Serves 4**

≋ This dish will improve on standing, either before or after cooking, so the flavours have time to blend.

Illustrated opposite

Top: **Broccoli and leek croustade** *(see above)*; Centre: **Piperade** *(see p. 57)*; Bottom: **Cottage pie with leeks and lentils** *(see above)*

Creamy onion flan

INGREDIENTS
100g (4 oz) wholewheat flour
pinch of salt
50g (2 oz) sunflower margarine or white vegetable fat and butter mixed
1 egg, beaten, plus a little milk or 30-45ml (2-3 tbsp) milk or soya milk
For the filling
15ml (1 tbsp) sunflower oil
225g (8 oz) onions, finely chopped
1 egg
30ml (2 tbsp) soured cream, cream cheese or thick yogurt
30ml (2 tbsp) chopped fresh parsley
pinch of grated nutmeg
salt and black pepper

Pastry made with egg or milk as the binding agent gives the best result in the microwave. Covering the pastry with absorbent paper and a plate ensures that all the moisture is absorbed and the pastry stays crisp.

1 Mix the flour and salt together in a bowl, then rub in the margarine or fat and butter until the mixture resembles fine breadcrumbs. Mix in the egg to form a smooth dough, adding a little milk if necessary. Alternatively use all milk or soya milk. Cover and leave to rest in a cool place for 15 mins.

2 Roll out the pastry and line a 20cm (8 in) flan dish. Prick the sides and base with a fork. Cover with absorbent paper and a plate and ≋ FULL for 5 mins. 600W *(4 mins. 700W; 6 mins. 500W)*, giving the dish a quarter turn every 1½ mins. Uncover and leave to cool.

3 For the filling, put the oil in a medium dish and ≋ FULL for 1 min. 600W *(30 secs. 700W; 1 min. 500W)*. Stir in the onions and ≋ FULL for 3 mins. 600W *(2½ mins. 700W; 3½ mins. 500W)*, stirring once or twice.

4 Cool slightly, then beat in the egg, soured cream, parsley and nutmeg. Season to taste with salt and pepper.

5 Pour the filling into the pastry case and ≋ FULL for 2½ mins. 600W *(2 mins. 700W; 3 mins. 500W)* until just set.

Preparation: 30 minutes

Cooking times: 11½ minutes

Power setting: FULL

Good reheated

Serves 4

Choose fillings that do not need much cooking once they are in the pastry case. Purées of lentils, split peas or vegetables such as parsnips are ideal.

Illustrated opposite

Flan Niçoise

INGREDIENTS
100g (4 oz) wholewheat flour
pinch of salt
30ml (2 tbsp) wheatgerm
50g (2 oz) sunflower margarine or white vegetable fat and butter mixed
15ml (1 tbsp) sunflower oil
For the filling
15ml (1 tbsp) olive oil
1 large onion, finely chopped
1-2 cloves garlic, crushed
175g (6 oz) mushrooms, diced
2 sticks celery, diced
200g (7 oz) can tomatoes, drained and mashed
12 black olives, stoned and minced
30ml (2 tbsp) tomato purée
5ml (1 tsp) green peppercorns
5ml (1 tsp) fresh marjoram
Garnish
2 tomatoes, sliced
6 black olives, stoned and halved

This flan filling is based on a traditional recipe from Southern France: well-cooked, soft vegetables with a rich tomato flavour enhanced with peppercorns, olives and herbs.

1 Mix the flour, salt and wheatgerm together. Rub in the margarine or fat and butter, then add the oil and 15-30ml (1-2 tbsp) water or milk. Mix to a smooth dough, then cover and leave to rest in a cool place for 15 mins.

2 Roll out the pastry and line a 20cm (8 in) flan dish. Cover with absorbent paper and a plate and ≋ FULL for 4 mins. 600W *(3-3½ mins. 700W; 5 mins. 500W)*. Uncover and leave to cool before filling.

3 For the filling, put the oil in a medium dish and ≋ FULL for 1 min. 600W *(30 secs. 700W; 1 min. 500W)*. Stir in the chopped onion and the crushed garlic and ≋ FULL for 1 min. 600W *(30 secs. 700W; 1 min. 500W)*.

4 Add the remaining ingredients with 30ml (2 tbsp) water. Cover and ≋ FULL for 5 mins. 600W *(4 mins. 700W; 6 mins. 500W)*, stirring once or twice. Season well with salt and pepper, then spoon the filling into the pastry case.

5 Garnish with tomatoes and olives and ≋ FULL for 5 mins. 600W *(4 mins. 700W; 6 mins. 500W)*, giving the dish a half turn halfway through.

Preparation: 35 minutes, plus cooling

Cooking time: 16 minutes

Power setting: FULL

Good reheated

Serves 4

The pastry case needs to be quite crisp before the filling is added. The wheatgerm enriches the dough and provides extra flavour.

Illustrated opposite

Top right: **Flan Niçoise** *(see above)*; Top left: **Creamy onion flan** *(see above)*; Bottom: **Scone pizza** *(see p. 63)*

Scone pizza

INGREDIENTS

150g (5 oz) self-raising wholewheat flour
pinch of salt
25g (1 oz) butter or margarine
1 egg, beaten
15ml (1 tbsp) skimmed milk

For the topping

15ml (1 tbsp) olive oil
2 small onions, finely chopped
1 clove garlic, crushed
2 medium tomatoes, skinned and chopped
15ml (1 tbsp) tomato purée
2.5ml (½ tsp) chopped fresh basil
5ml (1 tsp) dried oregano
5ml (1 tsp) green peppercorns or capers
50g (2 oz) cheese, grated

This pizza can be eaten either as a snack or as a full meal accompanied by a crisp, green salad. The scone base is very tasty and microwaves well. Make sure that the topping is well flavoured with garlic and herbs.

1   Mix the flour and salt together in a large bowl, then lightly rub in the butter or margarine. Add the beaten egg and milk and mix quickly to a soft dough.

2   Press the dough on to a 17.5cm (7 in) plate. Cover with greaseproof paper and an inverted plate and ≋ FULL for 4 mins. 600W *(3 mins. 700W; 5 mins. 500W)*, giving the plate a quarter turn every minute.

3   For the topping, put the oil in a medium dish and ≋ FULL for 1 min. 600W *(30 secs. 700W; 1 min. 500W)*. Stir in the chopped onions and garlic and ≋ FULL for 2 mins. 600W *(1½ mins. 700W; 2½ mins. 500W)*.

4   Add the tomatoes, tomato purée, herbs and green peppercorns or capers. Cover and ≋ FULL for 4 mins. 600W *(3 mins. 700W; 5 mins. 500W)*, stirring once or twice.

5   Spoon the topping over the base. Sprinkle with grated cheese and ≋ FULL for 2 mins. 600W *(1½ mins. 700W; 2½ mins. 500W)* until the cheese just melts. Alternatively, brown under a preheated conventional grill.

Preparation:
25 minutes

Cooking time:
13 minutes

Power setting:
FULL

**Serves 1-2, or
4 as a snack**

To skin tomatoes more easily, quickly heat them in the microwave. For two tomatoes, ≋ FULL for about 1 min. Remember to pierce or score the skins first.

Illustrated on p. 61

Crunchy Chinese vegetables

INGREDIENTS

225g (8 oz) carrots, cut into julienne strips
225g (8 oz) turnips, diced
225g (8 oz) mangetout, sliced
100g (4 oz) mooli (white radish), cut into julienne strips
salt and black pepper

For the sauce

15ml (1 tbsp) sunflower oil
1 clove garlic, crushed
2 spring onions, chopped
150ml (¼ pint) boiling vegetable stock
15ml (1 tbsp) wine vinegar
30ml (2 tbsp) honey
15ml (1 tbsp) shoyu
15ml (1 tbsp) sherry
100g (4 oz) fresh pineapple, grated
5ml (1 tsp) aniseed
10ml (2 tsp) arrowroot

This is a microwave version of a stir fry where the vegetables are cooked very quickly. The difference is that here the sauce is made before they are cooked and is used as a marinade.

1   Prepare all the vegetables and arrange in a large dish.

2   For the sauce, put the oil in a medium dish and ≋ FULL for 1 min. 600W *(30 secs. 700W; 1 min. 500W)*. Stir in the garlic and spring onions and ≋ FULL for 30 secs.

3   Add the remaining ingredients, except the arrowroot, and ≋ FULL for 3 mins. 600W *(2½ mins. 700W; 3½ mins. 500W)*, stirring once or twice.

4   Dissolve the arrowroot in a little water, then stir into the sauce. ≋ FULL for 2 mins. 600W *(1½ mins. 700W; 2½ mins. 500W)*, stirring once.

5   Pour the sauce over the vegetables, stir well, then cover and ≋ FULL for 5 mins *(4 mins. 700W; 6 mins 500W)*, stirring once or twice.

6   Leave to stand for 2 mins. then season to taste. Serve with noodles or rice.

Preparation:
25 minutes

Cooking time:
11½ minutes

Power setting:
FULL

Good reheated

Freezes well

Serves 4

Vary the ingredients according to the seasons, but always try to select ones that offer a range of colours.

Illustrated opposite

Opposite: **Crunchy Chinese vegetables** *(see above)*

Stuffed marrow

INGREDIENTS

1 medium marrow
100g (4 oz) brown or green lentils
900ml (1 ½ pints) boiling water
15ml (1 tbsp) sunflower oil
1 medium onion, finely chopped
2 sticks celery, diced
100g (4 oz) button mushrooms, diced
15ml (1 tbsp) tomato purèe
15-30ml (1-2 tbsp) shoyu
15ml (1 tbsp) chopped fresh parsley
5ml (1 tsp) chopped fresh thyme
salt and black pepper

Marrow can be a rather disappointing and watery vegetable if it is overcooked, but microwaved like this it retains a nutty, crunchy quality that complements the savoury filling.

1   Slice the marrow in half lengthways, then scoop out and discard the seeds. Remove a little of the flesh to leave a shell. Chop the flesh and reserve.

2   Put the lentils in a deep dish, pour over the boiling water, cover and ≋ FULL for 12-15 mins. (*all powers*) stirring several times. Leave to stand for 5 mins. then drain.

3   Put the oil in a medium dish and ≋ FULL for 1 min. 600W (*30 secs. 700W; 1 min. 500W*). Stir in the onion and ≋ FULL for 1 min. 600W (*30 secs. 700W; 1 min. 500W*).

4   Add the celery, mushrooms, marrow flesh and lentils. ≋ FULL for 2 mins. 600W (*1½ mins. 700W; 2½ mins. 500W*). Stir well, then cover and ≋ FULL for 6 mins. 600W (*5 mins. 700W; 7½ mins. 500W*), stirring once.

5   Stir in the tomato purée, shoyu and herbs. Season to taste with salt and pepper.

6   Pile the filling into the marrow shells, mounding it up well. Arrange in a large dish, cover and ≋ FULL for 8 mins. 600W (*6½ mins. 700W; 10 mins. 500W*), rearranging halfway through. Serve hot with a mushroom or tomato sauce.

★ **Preparation:** 25 minutes

≋ **Cooking time:** 30 minutes

∅ **Power setting:** FULL

◎ **Serves 4**

★ If preferred, use a large courgette or 2 smaller ones instead of a marrow.

Illustrated opposite

Creamy vegetable crumble

INGREDIENTS

25g (1 oz) sunflower margarine
1 medium onion, finely chopped
1 clove garlic, crushed
225g (8 oz) carrots, diced
225g (8 oz) peas
1 small cauliflower, divided into florets
30ml (2 tbsp) wholewheat flour
300ml (½ pint) skimmed milk
10ml (2 tsp) fines herbes
1 bay leaf
For the topping
50g (2 oz) oat flakes
50g (2 oz) buckwheat flour
25g (1 oz) wholewheat flour
15 ml (1 tbsp) chopped fresh parsley
50g (2 oz) sunflower margarine
30ml (2 tbsp) sunflower oil
5ml (1 tsp) shoyu

Buckwheat flour added to a microwave crumble mixture gives it a distinctive brown colour and makes it look more appetizing. The crumble is soft in texture but very tasty.

1   Put the margarine in a medium dish and ≋ FULL for 30 secs. Stir in the onion and garlic and ≋ FULL for 1 min. 600W (*30 secs. 700W; 1 min. 500W*).

2   Add the vegetables, cover and ≋ FULL for 5 mins. 600W (*4 mins. 700W; 6 mins. 500W*).

3   Stir in the flour and ≋ FULL for 30 secs. then stir in the milk, herbs and bay leaf. Re-cover and ≋ FULL for 2 mins. 600W (*1½ mins. 700W; 2½ mins. 500W*), then ≋ MEDIUM for 4 mins. 600W (*3 mins. 700W; ≋ DEFROST for 6 mins. 500W*), stirring once or twice.

4   For the topping, mix the flakes, flours and herbs together, then rub in the margarine. Stir in the oil and shoyu.

5   Cover the vegetables with the crumble topping and ≋ FULL for 8 mins. 600W (*6½ mins. 700W; 10 mins. 500W*), giving the dish a quarter turn every 2 mins.

6   Leave to stand for 2-3 mins. before serving.

★ **Preparation:** 15 minutes

≋ **Cooking time:** 21 minutes

∅ **Power settings:** FULL and MEDIUM

 Good reheated

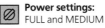 **Freezes well**

 Serves 4

≋ The sauce tends to bubble through during cooking, but if the dish stands for 2-3 mins. after cooking the top can be lightly forked over.

Illustrated opposite

Top: **Stuffed marrow** (*see above*); Bottom right: **Creamy vegetable crumble** (*see above*); Bottom left: **Layered courgette bake** (*see p. 66*)

Layered courgette bake

INGREDIENTS

6 medium courgettes
300ml (½ pint) skimmed milk
½ medium onion
1 bay leaf
1 blade of mace
sprig of thyme
sprig of parsley
25g (1 oz) sunflower margarine
25g (1 oz) wholewheat flour
2 spring onions, trimmed and chopped
225g (8 oz) frozen sweetcorn, thawed
2.5ml (½ tsp) grated nutmeg
salt and black pepper
Garnish (optional)
50-75g (2-3 oz) Cheddar cheese, grated

Courgette halves can be filled with a variety of sauces or vegetable mixtures. Cooked in the microwave, they keep their texture well and remain crisp and succulent.

1   Slice the courgettes in half lengthways. Place in a large dish, cover and ≋ FULL for 8 mins. 600W *(6½ mins. 700W; 10 mins. 500W)*, rearranging halfway through. Scoop out the flesh, leaving a shell, and chop finely. Set aside.

2   Put the milk, onion, bay leaf, mace and herbs in a jug and ≋ FULL for 3 mins. 600W *(2½ mins. 700W; 3½ mins. 500W)*. Leave to stand for 5 mins. then strain.

3   Put the margarine in a medium dish and ≋ FULL for 30 secs. Stir in the flour and ≋ FULL for 30 secs.

4   Pour in the infused milk, stirring well. ≋ FULL for 2-3 mins. 600W *(1½-2½ mins. 700W; 2½-3½ mins. 500W)*, stirring 2-3 times to keep a smooth consistency.

5   Mix the spring onions, sweetcorn, courgette flesh and nutmeg into the white sauce. Season with salt and pepper.

6   Arrange half the courgettes in the bottom of a deep dish. Cover with half the sauce, then top with the remaining courgettes. Pour over the remaining sauce and ≋ FULL for 5 mins. 600W *(4 mins. 700W; 6 mins. 500W)*, giving the dish a quarter turn every 1½ mins.

7   When adding cheese, sprinkle it over the top 3 mins. before the end of the cooking time. If preferred, brown the dish under a preheated conventional grill before serving.

★ **Preparation:**
20 minutes

≈ **Cooking time:**
19 minutes

⊘ **Power setting:**
FULL

≋ **Good reheated**

◎ **Serves 6**

Illustrated on p. 65

Vegetable gado gado

INGREDIENTS

100g (4 oz) peanuts
30ml (2 tbsp) groundnut oil
1 onion finely chopped
1 clove garlic, crushed
1 bay leaf
5ml (1 tsp) grated fresh root ginger
1 green chilli, diced
juice of 1 lemon
15ml (1 tbsp) honey
300ml (½ pint) boiling light stock
15ml (1 tbsp) shoyu
salt and black pepper
For the vegetables
4 spring onions, diced
225g (8 oz) mangetout, sliced
100g (4 oz) mooli, diced
2 red peppers, diced
350g (12 oz) green beans

The rich peanut sauce is quick and easy to make in the microwave. The vegetables should be crunchy but hot, so serve them as soon as they are cooked.

1   Spread out the peanuts in a shallow dish and ≋ FULL for 3 mins. 600W *(2½ mins. 700W; 3½ mins. 500W)*, shaking the dish halfway through. Grind to a fine powder.

2   Put the oil in a medium dish and ≋ FULL for 1½ mins. 600W *(1 min. 700W; 1½ mins. 500W)*. Stir in the onion and garlic and ≋ FULL for 1 min. 600W *(30 secs. 700W; 1 min. 500W)*.

3 Add the remaining ingredients, including the ground nuts. Season to taste with salt and pepper, and ≋ FULL for 8 mins. 600W *(6½ mins. 700W; 10 mins. 500W)*, stirring 3-4 times.

4   Prepare all the vegetables and slice them finely. Mix together in a large dish and add 30ml (2 tbsp) water. Cover and ≋ FULL for 4 mins. 600W *(3 mins. 700W; 5 mins. 500W)*, stirring once or twice.

5   Pour the sauce over the vegetables and serve with brown rice, pot barley or wholemeal noodles.

★ **Preparation:**
25 minutes

≈ **Cooking time:**
17½ minutes

⊘ **Power setting:**
FULL

≋ **Good reheated**

◎ **Serves 4**

Illustrated opposite

Top: **Vegetable gado gado** *(see above)*; Bottom: **Marinaded tofu with vegetables** *(see p. 68)*

Marinaded tofu with vegetables

INGREDIENTS

225g (8 oz) firm tofu, cut into
2.5cm (1 in) squares

For the marinade

75ml (3 fl oz) red wine

30ml (2 tbsp) shoyu

15ml (1 tbsp) concentrated
apple juice

15ml (1 tbsp) mild mustard
powder

2.5ml (½ tsp) chopped fresh
rosemary

2.5ml (½ tsp) chopped
fresh sage

1 clove garlic, crushed

For the vegetable
accompaniment

15ml (1 tbsp) sunflower oil

350g (12 oz) leeks, cut into
chunks

225g (8 oz) broccoli, divided
into florets

100g (4 oz) turnips, cut into
julienne strips

100g (4 oz) carrots, cut into
julienne strips

salt and black pepper

The microwave is ideal for making quick marinades. Tofu benefits greatly from being marinaded as it acts like blotting paper, soaking up all the flavours of the marinade ingredients. Use firm or regular tofu which slices easily and does not fall apart during cooking.

1   Mix the marinade ingredients together in a shallow dish. Add the tofu, baste well, cover and ≋ FULL for 3 mins. 600W *(2½ mins. 700W; 3½ mins. 500W),* stirring once. Leave to stand for 10-15 mins.

2   For the vegetables, put the oil in a medium dish and ≋ FULL for 1 min. 600W *(30 secs. 700W; 1 min. 500W).* Stir in the chopped leeks and ≋ FULL for 2 mins. 600W *(1½ mins. 700W; 2½ mins. 500W).*

3   Add the broccoli, turnips and carrots. Cover and ≋ FULL for 2 mins. 600W *(1½ mins. 700W; 2½ mins. 500W).*

4   Add 30ml (2 tbsp) of the marinade, re-cover and ≋ FULL for 4-5 mins. 600W *(3-4 mins. 700W; 5-6 mins. 600W),* stirring once. Leave to stand for 2 mins. then season to taste with salt and pepper.

5   Meanwhile reheat the tofu, cover and ≋ FULL for 2 mins. 600W *(1½ mins. 700W; 2½ mins. 500W).*

6   Serve with the vegetables and brown rice, either mixing the tofu with the vegetables or keeping them separate.

 Preparation:
25 minutes

 Cooking time:
14 minutes

Power setting:
FULL

≋ **Good reheated**

◎ **Serves 4**

≋ The cooking time in this recipe produces crisp vegetables, cook for longer if a softer texture is preferred.

Illustrated on p. 67

VEGETABLE SIDE DISHES

Vegetables are delicious cooked in the microwave. They retain their fresh taste, colour and texture, and their nutritional value is less likely to be destroyed by microwave cooking than by conventional methods. Only use fresh, undamaged vegetables; the microwave will not be able to improve or soften tough, old, withered or blemished specimens. Always underestimate the cooking time required as they will continue to cook and soften for several minutes after they have been removed from the oven. Mix vegetables for their complementary tastes, colours and textures. Enhance their flavours further with exotic spices as in Spiced Cauliflower and Hungarian Marrow. Mix them with refreshing and unusual sauce combinations or make into purées enriched with soft cheeses, yogurt or eggs. Adapt the recipes according to the vegetables you have available and serve them as side dishes or in combination with cooked grains, pulses, pasta or pastry to make a more substantial meal.

Braised red cabbage

INGREDIENTS

15ml (1 tbsp) sunflower oil
1 onion, sliced into rings
1 clove garlic, crushed
175g (6 oz) fennel or celery, diced
5ml (1 tsp) fennel or caraway seeds
450g (1 lb) red cabbage, shredded
50g (2 oz) raisins
45ml (3 tbsp) red wine
15ml (1 tbsp) honey
salt and black pepper

Using the microwave is a marvellously quick way to make this delicious vegetable side dish. Try adding nuts, walnuts or extra fruit, such as fresh apple or dried apricots.

1   Put the oil in a medium dish and ≈ FULL for 1 min. 600W *(30 secs. 700W; 1 min. 500W)*. Stir in the sliced onion and the garlic and ≈ FULL for 2 mins. 600W *(1½ mins. 700W; 2½ mins. 500W)*.

2   Add the fennel or celery, the seeds and 15ml (1 tbsp) water. Cover and ≈ FULL for 4 mins. 600W *(3 mins. 700W; 5 mins. 500W)*, stirring once.

3   Stir in the remaining ingredients, except the seasoning, re-cover and ≈ FULL for 10 mins. 600W *(8½ mins. 700W; 12½ mins. 500W)*, stirring 3 times.

4   Leave to stand for 3 mins., then season well with salt and pepper. Serve hot or cold.

★ **Preparation:**
20 minutes

≈ **Cooking time:**
17 minutes

∅ **Power setting:**
FULL

≋ **Good reheated**

◎ **Serves 4**

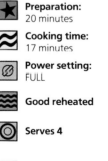 ≈ To produce cabbage with a slightly softer texture, cook for a few minutes longer than the time in this recipe.

Illustrated on p. 70

Broccoli with olives and garlic

INGREDIENTS

15ml (1 tbsp) olive oil
1 small onion, finely chopped
350g (12 oz) broccoli, divided into small, even-sized florets
8-12 large olives, stoned
1 medium tomato
15ml (1 tbsp) red wine vinegar
1 clove garlic
2.5ml (½ tsp) garam masala
salt and black pepper

The pungent olive and tomato sauce with garlic and spices gives the broccoli a rich and exotic flavour. Everything is heated so quickly that the broccoli remains crisp yet tender. Serve it with pasta shapes, such as rigatoni, and freshly grated Parmesan cheese to make a delicious main dish.

1 Put the oil in a medium dish and ≈ FULL for 1 min. 600W *(30 secs. 700W; 1 min. 500W)*. Stir in the onion and ≈ FULL for 2 mins. 600W *(1½ mins. 700W, 2½ mins. 500W)*.

2 Stir in the broccoli, then add 30ml (2 tbsp) water. Cover and ≈ FULL for 5 mins. 600W *(4 mins. 700W; 6 mins. 500W)*, stirring once. Leave to stand for 2-3 mins.

3 Meanwhile, liquidize the olives, tomato, vinegar, garlic and garam masala to make a coarse-textured sauce.

4 Drain the vegetables, then toss in the sauce. Cover and ≈ FULL for 1 min. to reheat. Season well with salt and pepper. Serve hot or cold.

 Preparation: 20 minutes

Cooking time: 8 minutes

Power setting: FULL

Serves 4

Illustrated opposite

Creamy carrot and parsnip bake

INGREDIENTS

450g (1 lb) mixed carrots and parsnips, diced
75g (3 oz) quark
10ml (2 tsp) sesame oil
salt and black pepper
15-30ml (1-2 tbsp) sesame seeds

Mixtures of mashed root vegetables are always popular, and using quark gives this vegetable purée a lovely creamy flavour. The quick cooking time retains the fresh taste of the vegetables.

1 Put the carrots and parsnips in a large bowl with 30ml (2 tbsp) water. Cover and ≈ FULL for 5 mins. 600W *(4 mins. 700W; 6 mins. 500W)*. Leave to stand for 2-3 mins. to finish cooking then drain.

2 Liquidize the carrots and parsnips with the quark and sesame oil, then season well with salt and pepper.

3 Sprinkle the sesame seeds thickly over the base of a small dish and ≈ FULL for 2 mins. 600W *(1½ mins. 700W; 2½ mins. 500W)*, shaking the dish halfway through.

4 Spread the purée over the top of the seeds, then ≈ FULL for 30 secs. to reheat. Turn out and serve in wedges.

Preparation: 15 minutes

Cooking time: 7½ minutes

Power setting: FULL

Serves 4

 Make the purée with a mixture of carrots and swede instead of parsnip, if preferred.

Illustrated opposite

Top: **Broccoli with olives and garlic** *(see above)*; Centre: **Braised red cabbage** *(see p. 69)*; Bottom: **Creamy carrot and parsnip bake** *(see above)*

Hungarian marrow

There is no need to add any extra water when cooking the marrow for this recipe so its texture remains firm and crisp, and the full flavours of the ingredients are absorbed.

1   Peel the marrow if the skin is tough or the marrow a little old, otherwise leave it on. Slice the marrow in half, discard the seeds and chop the flesh into 1cm (½ in) cubes. The flesh should weigh about 450-700g (1-1½ lb).

2   Put the oil and garlic in a medium dish and ≈ FULL for 2 mins. 600W *(1½ mins. 700W; 2½ mins. 500W)*. Add the marrow and paprika and ≈ FULL for 2 mins. 600W *(1½ mins. 700W; 2½ mins. 500W)*.

3   Add the wine, dill weed and cayenne. Stir well, cover and ≈ FULL for 3 mins. 600W *(2½ mins. 700W; 3½ mins. 500W)*, stirring halfway through.

4   Season to taste with salt and pepper. Serve hot or cold.

INGREDIENTS

450-700g (1-1½ lb) marrow
15ml (1 tbsp) sunflower oil
1 clove garlic, crushed
5ml (1 tsp) paprika
30ml (2 tbsp) white wine
5ml (1 tsp) dill weed
pinch of cayenne
salt

★ **Preparation:** 15 minutes

≈ **Cooking time:** 7 minutes

⊘ **Power setting:** FULL

◎ **Serves 4**

★ Substitute courgettes when marrows are out of season.

Illustrated opposite

Green bean, mushroom and artichoke medley

Liven up different assortments of cooked vegetables with tasty sauces like this tomato-based one, which can be heated through in seconds. The speed of the cooking means that the sauce is not absorbed by the vegetables, it simply highlights and complements their individual flavours.

1   Put the beans in a large bowl with 30ml (2 tbsp) water, cover and ≈ FULL for 5 mins. 600W *(4 mins. 700W; 6 mins. 500W)*, stirring once.

2   Add the mushrooms and artichoke hearts. Re-cover and ≈ FULL for 3 mins. 600W *(2½ mins. 700W; 3½ mins. 500W)*. Drain, reserving the liquid to be used as stock.

3   Liquidize the tomato, tomato purée, onion, garlic, shoyu and stock until smooth.

4   Stir the sauce into the vegetables. Cover and ≈ FULL for 1 min. then season well with salt and pepper. Serve hot or cold.

INGREDIENTS

350g (12 oz) green beans, trimmed and sliced in half
100g (4 oz) button mushrooms, quartered
100g (4 oz) artichoke hearts, halved
1 medium tomato
15ml (1 tbsp) tomato purée
1 small onion, finely chopped
1 clove garlic, crushed
15ml (1 tbsp) shoyu
25ml (1 fl oz) stock
salt and black pepper

★ **Preparation:** 15 minutes

≈ **Cooking time:** 9 minutes

⊘ **Power setting:** FULL

◎ **Serves 4**

Illustrated opposite

Top: **Hungarian marrow** *(see above)*; Centre: **Green bean, mushroom and artichoke medley** *(see above)*; Bottom: **Spiced cauliflower** *(see p. 75)*

Spiced cauliflower

INGREDIENTS

7.5ml (1½ tsp) sesame seeds
7.5ml (1½ tsp) cumin seeds
7.5ml (1½ tsp) mustard seeds
15ml (1 tbsp) sesame oil
1 onion, finely chopped
1 clove garlic, crushed
1 small cauliflower, divided into small, even-sized florets
150ml (¼ pint) yogurt
salt and black pepper

Cauliflower cooked by this method in the microwave retains the crisp texture and nutty flavour of the raw vegetable. The mixture of aromatic spices gives extra flavour and transforms it into an unusual side dish, which goes particulary well with the pilaff recipes on pages 45 and 46.

1 Put the seeds on a small plate and ≋ FULL for 1 min. 600W *(30 secs. 700W; 1 min. 500W)* to develop their flavour. Grind to a powder.

2 Put the oil in a medium dish and ≋ FULL for 1 min. 600W *(30 secs. 700W; 1 min. 500W)*. Stir in the chopped onion and the garlic and ≋ FULL for 2 mins. 600W *(1½ mins. 700W; 2½ mins. 500W)*.

3 Add the cauliflower florets, seeds and 15ml (1 tbsp) water, stir well, then cover and ≋ FULL for 2 mins. 600W *(1½ mins. 700W; 2½ mins. 500W)*.

4 Stir in the yogurt, then re-cover and ≋ LOW for 2 mins. 600W *(1½ mins. 700W; ≋ DEFROST for 2 mins. 500W)*. It is important that the yogurt doesn't boil or it will curdle.

5 Season well with salt and pepper. Serve hot or cold.

★ **Preparation:** 15 minutes

≋ **Cooking time:** 7½ minutes

∅ **Power settings:** FULL and LOW

◎ **Serves 4**

★ Chop the cauliflower stalk into small pieces and use to make up a vegetable stock or soup.

Illustrated on p. 73

Hot green salad

INGREDIENTS

15ml (1 tbsp) olive oil
4 spring onions, trimmed and chopped
4 sticks celery, diced
½ avocado, peeled and diced
1 green pepper, deseeded and diced
1 Cos lettuce, chopped
½ cucumber, diced
For the dressing
5ml (1 tsp) mustard powder
15ml (1 tbsp) white wine vinegar
30ml (2 tbsp) olive oil
10ml (2 tsp) chopped fresh herbs e.g. chives and basil
salt and black pepper

An unusual idea for a side salad that is only possible with a microwave. The salad ingredients remain crisp, but the avocado melts to give an extra buttery flavour to the dressing. This dish also makes a delicious starter.

1 Put the oil in a medium dish and ≋ FULL for 1 min. 600W *(30 secs. 700W; 1 min. 500W)*.

2 Stir in the spring onions and ≋ FULL for 1 min. 600W *(30 secs. 700W; 1 min. 500W)*.

3 Add all the salad ingredients.

4 Mix all the dressing ingredients together and toss into the salad. Cover and ≋ FULL for 3 mins. 600W *(2½ mins. 700W; 3½ mins. 500W)*.

5 Toss the salad, then leave to stand for 2 mins. Serve hot.

★ **Preparation:** 20 minutes

≋ **Cooking time:** 5 minutes

∅ **Power setting:** FULL

◎ **Serves 4**

Illustrated opposite

Opposite: **Hot green salad** *(see above)*

Marinaded peppers

INGREDIENTS

4 medium peppers, preferably
2 red, 1 yellow and 1 green

salt

For the marinade

90ml (6 tbsp) olive oil

30ml (2 tbsp) red wine vinegar

5ml (1 tsp) grain mustard

10ml (2 tsp) capers, chopped

15ml (1 tbsp) finely chopped
fresh parsley

5ml (1 tsp) chopped fresh
thyme

1-2 cloves garlic, crushed

black pepper

For the garnish

15ml (1 tbsp) finely chopped
fresh parsley

This is a rich, tasty idea for an interesting starter or a salad accompaniment. The salad can be made with aubergines instead of peppers.

1   Slit the skin of the peppers, then arrange on a plate, and ≋ FULL for 15 mins. 600W *(12½ mins. 700W; 19 mins. 500W)*, turning over and rearranging halfway through. Drop the peppers into a bowl of cold water, leave for 5 mins., then remove the skin and deseed.

2   Cut each pepper into four or six pieces and place in a small deep dish.

3   Mix the marinade ingredients together and pour over the peppers. Cover and ≋ FULL for 2 mins. 600W *(1½ mins. 700W; 2½ mins. 500W)*.

4   Leave until cold, then season to taste with salt. Serve straight from the dish or drain the peppers and place on individual plates. Garnish with parsley.

 Preparation:
20 minutes

Cooking time:
18 minutes

Power setting:
FULL

Serves 4

It doesn't matter if the peppers collapse a little during the microwaving, they need to be well cooked in order to remove the skin.

Illustrated opposite

Braised fennel
in tomato and apricot sauce

INGREDIENTS

700g (1½ lb) fennel bulbs,
trimmed

For the sauce

15ml (1 tbsp) olive oil

1 medium onion, finely
chopped

1 clove garlic, crushed

25g (1 oz) dried apricots, cut
into slivers

400g (14 oz) can tomatoes,
mashed

15ml (1 tbsp) tomato purée

15ml (1 tbsp) chopped fennel
fronds or 2.5ml (½ tsp)
fennel seeds

salt and black pepper

Fennel cooked in the microwave retains its delicate flavour, and the texture remains pleasantly crunchy. To make a more substantial dish, cover with grated cheese and brown under a conventional grill, or serve with pasta and Parmesan cheese or chopped nuts.

1   For the sauce, put the oil in a medium dish and ≋ FULL for 1 min. 600W *(30 secs. 700W; 1 min. 500W)*. Stir in the chopped onion and garlic and ≋ FULL for 1 min. 600W *(30 secs. 700W; 1 min. 500W)*.

2   Add the apricots, tomatoes, tomato purée and fennel fronds or seeds. Cover and ≋ FULL for 10 mins. 600W *(8½ mins. 700W; 12½ mins. 500W)*, stirring several times.

3   Slice the fennel into four chunks, or if using two bulbs, slice each one into four.

4   Arrange the fennel in a shallow dish, add 30ml (2 tbsp) water, cover and ≋ FULL for 6 mins. 600W *(5 mins. 700W; 7½ mins. 500W)*, turning once or twice. Cook for longer if a softer vegetable is preferred. Drain, reserving the liquid.

5   Add the cooking liquid to the tomato sauce, then liquidize until smooth. Season well with salt and pepper.

6   Pour the sauce over the fennel in the dish and ≋ FULL for 1 min. to reheat. Serve hot.

 Preparation:
20 minutes

Cooking time:
19 minutes

 Power setting:
FULL

Serves 4

Illustrated opposite

Top left: **Cheese and potato layer** *(see p. 78)*; Top right: **Marinaded peppers** *(see above)*; Bottom right: **Marinaded beef tomatoes** *(see p. 78)*; Bottom left: **Braised fennel in tomato and apricot sauce** *(see above)*

Marinaded beef tomatoes

INGREDIENTS

15ml (1 tbsp) olive oil
3 spring onions, finely chopped
1 clove garlic, crushed
50g (2 oz) fennel, chopped, or 5ml (1 tsp) fennel seeds
45ml (3 tbsp) red wine
30ml (2 tbsp) tomato purée
5ml (1 tsp) shoyu
5ml (1 tsp) chopped fresh tarragon
450g (1 lb) beef tomatoes
30ml (2 tbsp) chopped fresh parsley
salt and black pepper

The large Italian beef tomatoes make a delicious side vegetable or starter. Their flavour is enhanced with this simple marinade, which is easy and quick to make using the microwave.

1   Put the oil in a medium dish and ≋ FULL for 1 min. 600W *(30 secs. 700W; 1 min. 500W).*

2   Stir in the onions, garlic and fennel or fennel seeds and ≋ FULL for 30 secs.

3   Mix in the wine, tomato purée, shoyu and tarragon. Add a little more olive oil if the dressing is too sharp.

4   Slice the tomatoes and lay them in the dressing, basting well. Sprinkle with parsley, cover and ≋ FULL for 5 mins. 600W *(4 mins. 700W; 6 mins. 500W).*

5   Season with salt and pepper and serve hot or chilled.

 Preparation: 10 minutes

 Cooking time: 6½ minutes

 Power setting: FULL

 Serves 4

Illustrated on p. 77

Cheese and potato layer

INGREDIENTS

175g (6 oz) Cheddar cheese, grated
550g (1¼ lb) potatoes, scrubbed and thinly sliced
225g (8 oz) onions, cut into thin rings
5ml (1 tsp) chopped fresh sage
5ml (1 tsp) chopped fresh thyme
150ml (¼ pint) skimmed milk
1.25ml (¼ tsp) grated nutmeg
salt and black pepper

This dish could be served as a side vegetable with a rich stew or on its own as an easy supper snack. It is best finished off under a conventional grill so that the cheese is golden and bubbling.

1   Set aside 25g (1 oz) of the cheese for the topping. Layer the potatoes, onions and cheese in a medium dish, sprinkling the herbs over each of the layers. Finish with a layer of cheese.

2   Mix the milk and nutmeg together and season well with salt and pepper.

3   Pour the milk over the vegetables and cheese, cover and ≋ FULL for 15 mins. 600W *(12½ mins. 700W; 17-18 mins. 500W),* giving the dish a quarter turn every 5 mins.

4   Leave to stand for 4 mins. Sprinkle with the reserved cheese and melt under a preheated conventional grill. Serve hot.

★ Preparation: 30 minutes

≋ Cooking time: 15 minutes

⊘ Power setting: FULL

 Good reheated

✳ Freezes well

◎ Serves 4

★ Add other vegetables or cooked beans to make a more substantial dish.

Illustrated on p. 77

Runner beans with walnut sauce

INGREDIENTS

450g (1 lb) runner beans, trimmed and cut into 2.5cm (1 in) lengths

For the sauce

15g (½ oz) sunflower margarine
15g (½ oz) wholewheat flour
150ml (¼ pint) skimmed milk
50g (2 oz) chopped walnuts
salt and black pepper

Fresh runner beans are a true sign of summer. Their strong flavour goes particularly well with this creamy sauce enriched with crunchy walnut pieces.

1   Put the beans in a large bowl with 45ml (3 tbsp) water. Cover and ≋ FULL for 5 mins. 600W *(4 mins. 700W; 6 mins. 500W)*. Strain, reserving the liquid. Make up the liquid to 150ml (¼ pint) with water.

2   Put the margarine in a medium dish and ≋ FULL for 30 secs. Stir in the flour and ≋ FULL for 30 secs.

3   Stir in the milk and the bean cooking water. Cover and ≋ FULL for 4 mins. 600W *(3 mins. 700W; 5 mins. 500W)*, stirring several times.

4   Stir in the chopped walnuts and season well with salt and pepper. Pour the sauce over the beans and ≋ FULL for 30 secs. to reheat. Serve hot.

★ **Preparation:**
15 minutes

≋ **Cooking time:**
10½ minutes

∅ **Power setting:**
FULL

◎ **Serves 4**

★ Any variety of green bean can be used instead of runner beans, if preferred.

Illustrated on p. 80

Spinach cream

INGREDIENTS

450g (1 lb) spinach
100g (4 oz) cottage cheese
50g (2 oz) cream cheese
1 egg
2.5ml (½ tsp) grated nutmeg
salt and black pepper

This dish makes a delicious starter, or a light meal when served with a tomato salad and wholemeal rolls. Use 175g (6 oz) ricotta in place of the cottage cheese and cream cheese mixture if you prefer.

1   Wash the spinach and shred finely. Place in a medium dish, cover and ≋ FULL for 2 mins. 600W *(1½ mins. 700W; 2½ mins. 500W)*.

2   Drain the spinach, then liquidize until smooth. Add the cheeses and blend until smooth. Beat in the egg and the nutmeg. Season well with salt and pepper.

3   Divide the mixture between four ramekin dishes, then ≋ FULL for 3 mins. 600W *(2½ mins. 700W; 3½ mins. 500W)*. The cream should still be soft at this stage—do not cook until firm or the texture will become rubbery. Serve hot.

★ **Preparation:**
15 minutes

≋ **Cooking time:**
5 minutes

∅ **Power setting:**
FULL

◎ **Serves 4**

★ Plain spinach cooks beautifully in the microwave, especially if you buy young tender leaves which can be cooked in seconds. The water that clings to the leaves after washing is sufficient to cook the spinach.

Illustrated on p. 80

Baby beetroots with orange sauce

INGREDIENTS

350g (12 oz) uncooked baby beetroots, scrubbed

For the sauce

150ml (¼ pint) orange juice
juice of ½ lemon
15ml (1 tbsp) concentrated apple juice
1cm (½ in) fresh root ginger, grated
1.25ml (¼ tsp) celery seeds
7.5ml (1½ tsp) arrowroot

Hot beetroot is just as delicious as cold, but it needs a sauce to balance its slightly dry texture, and the sweetness of orange juice is perfect.

1   Pierce each beetroot once or twice, then arrange around the edge of a medium dish, evenly spacing each one. Cover and ≋ FULL for 8 mins. 600W *(6½ mins. 700W; 10 mins. 500W)*, rearranging twice during the cooking time. Leave to stand for 3 mins. then peel, if wished.

2   Meanwhile, mix all the sauce ingredients together, except the arrowroot, in a medium dish. ≋ FULL for 2 mins. 600W *(1½ mins. 700W; 2½ mins. 500W)*, stirring several times.

3   Dissolve the arrowroot in a little water, then stir into the sauce. ≋ FULL for 2 mins. 600W *(1½ mins. 700W; 2½ mins. 500W)* until the liquid boils and clears.

4   Pour the sauce over the beetroot and serve hot. Garnish with parsley for extra colour.

★	**Preparation:** 15 minutes
≋	**Cooking time:** 12 minutes
⌀	**Power setting:** FULL
≋	**Good reheated**
◎	**Serves 4**

Illustrated opposite

Ratatouille

INGREDIENTS

15ml (1 tbsp) olive oil
1 medium onion, finely chopped
1 clove garlic, crushed
1 aubergine, weighing about 225g (8 oz), diced
225g (8 oz) courgettes, diced
1 medium green or red pepper, deseeded and diced
400g (14 oz) can tomatoes
15ml (1 tbsp) tomato purée
10ml (2 tsp) chopped fresh thyme
5ml (1 tsp) chopped fresh marjoram
1 bay leaf
salt and pepper

Vegetable stews such as ratatouille work very well in the microwave. They are simple to prepare, the texture remains good and the flavours infuse into the sauce.

1   Put the oil in a medium dish and ≋ FULL for 1 min. 600W *(30 secs. 700W; 1 min. 500W)*.

2   Stir in the chopped onion and the garlic and ≋ FULL for 2 mins. 600W *(1½ mins. 700W; 2½ mins. 500W)*.

3   Add the diced aubergine, courgettes and pepper. ≋ FULL for 3 mins. 600W *(2½ mins. 700W; 3½ mins. 500W)*.

4   Add the remaining ingredients, except the seasoning, stir well, then cover and ≋ FULL for 8 mins. 600W *(6½ mins. 700W; 10 mins. 500W)*, stirring once or twice.

5   Season to taste with salt and pepper and serve hot.

★	**Preparation:** 20 minutes
≋	**Cooking time:** 14 minutes
⌀	**Power setting:** FULL
≋	**Good reheated**
◎	**Serves 4**

★ Other combinations of vegetables can be used in this recipe—try fresh broad beans, green beans and mushrooms.

Illustrated opposite

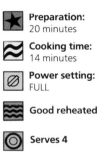

Clockwise from the top: **Runner beans with walnut sauce** *(see p. 79)*; **Baby beetroots with orange sauce** *(see above)*; **Spinach cream** *(see p. 79)*; **Ratatouille** *(see above)*

Barbecue-style baked potatoes

INGREDIENTS

100g (4 oz) pinto beans, soaked overnight
900ml (1½ pints) boiling water
4 large potatoes
For the sauce
225ml (8 fl oz) tomato juice
45ml (3 tbsp) red wine
60ml (4 tbsp) lemon juice
30ml (2 tbsp) wine vinegar
30ml (2 tbsp) concentrated apple juice
100g (4 oz) mushrooms, diced
2 sticks celery
30ml (2 tbsp) chopped fresh parsley
5ml (1 tsp) chopped fresh thyme
salt and black pepper

It's easy to make a wholesome meal out of a baked potato by mixing the flesh with a selection of ingredients. Here are four of my favourite fillings, all of which cook beautifully by microwave. You can speed up this first recipe by using pre-cooked beans.

1 Drain the beans and place in a deep bowl. Pour over the boiling water. Ensure that it covers the beans by 3-5cm (1-2 in). Add more if necessary. Cover and ≋ FULL for 25 mins. 600W *(21 mins. 700W; 30 mins. 500W)* until just soft. Drain.

2 Pierce each potato, wrap in absorbent paper and ≋ FULL for 15 mins. 600W *(12½ mins. 700W; 18 mins. 500W)*, turning over and rearranging halfway through. Stand for 5 mins.

3 For the sauce, mix all the ingredients together, then stir into the cooked beans.

4 Slice the potatoes in half and scoop out the flesh. Mix with the beans and sauce. Fill the potato halves with the mixture, piling it up into a mound.

5 Arrange the potato halves on a plate and ≋ FULL for 3 mins. 600W *(2½ mins. 700W; 3½ mins. 500W)* or until heated through, rearranging once.

  Preparation: 15 minutes

 Cooking time: 43 minutes

Power setting: FULL

≋ Good reheated

◎ Serves 4

★ Use cider vinegar instead of wine vinegar if preferred. Red kidney beans can be used instead of pinto beans, but they should be boiled on the top of the stove for 10 minutes before cooking in the microwave.

Illustrated opposite

VARIATIONS
Leek and horseradish filling

INGREDIENTS

225g (8 oz) leeks, finely chopped
30-45ml (2-3 tbsp) water
5ml (1 tsp) horseradish sauce
30ml (2 tbsp) yogurt
salt and black pepper
2 baked potatoes

1 Put the leeks in a medium dish with the water. Cover and ≋ FULL for 3 mins. 600W *(2½ mins. 700W; 3½ mins. 500W)*, stirring once. Drain well.

2 Liquidize the leeks with the horseradish and yogurt. Season to taste with salt and pepper.

3 Scoop out a little of the potato flesh, add to the purée, then spoon back into the potatoes.

4 ≋ FULL for 2 mins. 600W *(1½ mins. 700W; 2½ mins. 500W)* or until hot.

 ◎ Fills 2 potatoes

★ To bake 2 potatoes, follow the same method as above but bake for 8 mins. 600W *(7 mins. 700W; 10 mins. 500W)*, remembering to turn over and rearrange halfway through. Leave for 3-4 mins. to soften.

Illustrated opposite

Peanut and yogurt filling

INGREDIENTS

15ml (1 tbsp) peanut butter
15ml (1 tbsp) yogurt
5ml (1 tsp) shoyu
2 baked potatoes

1 Cream the ingredients together.

2 Halve the baked potatoes and scoop out some of the flesh. Combine with the sauce and spoon back into the potato cases.

3 ≋ FULL for 3 mins. 600W *(2½ mins. 700W; 3½ mins. 500W)*.

 ◎ Fills 2 potatoes

Illustrated opposite

Cheese filling

INGREDIENTS

50g (2 oz) cheese, grated
25g (1 oz) margarine
2.5ml (½ tsp) caraway seeds
2.5ml (½ tsp) mustard seeds
black pepper
2 baked potatoes

1 Beat the cheese and margarine together in a small dish, then add the remaining ingredients.

2 Scoop out a little of the potato flesh, and add to the cheese mixture. Spoon the filling into the hot potatoes, then ≋ FULL for 2 mins. 600W *(1½ mins. 700W; 2½ mins. 500W)*.

 ◎ Fills 2 potatoes

Illustrated opposite

Clockwise from top right: **Barbecue-style baked potato** *(see above)*; **Leek and horseradish filling** *(see above)*; **Peanut and yogurt filling** *(see above)*; **Cheese filling** *(see above)*

SAUCES AND PRESERVES

All sauces, whether savoury or sweet, stock-based or milk-based, cook wonderfully well in the microwave. They are not much quicker than by conventional methods but they are much less hazardous. Lumps are unlikely to form provided you stir the mixture frequently, and there is no risk of burning or sticking as direct heat is not involved. Cook sauces in the bowls or jugs you plan to serve them in to eliminate messy washing up. Make them in advance for freezing or refrigerating and simply reheat as required while other foods are standing. Preserves and chutneys are very easy to make in small quanitites in the microwave and you avoid filling the house with the lingering smells of vinegar and spices. Cook them in containers two or three times larger than the volume being made to avoid spillage as the mixture will bubble up considerably. Make different varieties at frequent intervals so you can ring the changes and take advantage of what's in season. The fruit preserves do not keep as long as traditional high-sugar jams, but they will keep in the fridge for between two and three weeks or in the freezer, and have a delicious, fresh flavour.

Concentrated vegetable stock

INGREDIENTS

15ml (1 tbsp) sunflower oil
½ medium onion, with the skin left on
1 medium carrot, chopped in large chunks
100g (4 oz) leeks, chopped
handful of celery leaves
1.25ml (¼ tsp) celery seeds
sprig of parsley and thyme

Make a strongly flavoured stock using less water—anything cooked with a high proportion of water doesn't save much time in the microwave. Dilute the stock to taste when using in soups and sauces.

1 Put the oil in a deep bowl and ≈ FULL for 1 min. 600W (*30 secs. 700W; 1 min. 500W*).

2 Stir in the vegetables and celery seeds and ≈ FULL for 3 mins. 600W (*2½ mins. 700W; 3½ mins. 500W*), stirring once or twice.

3 Add 600ml (1 pint) water and herbs. Cover and ≈ FULL for 12 mins. 600W (*10 mins. 700W; 15 mins. 500W*).

4 Strain, season and dilute as required.

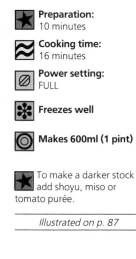

Preparation:
10 minutes

Cooking time:
16 minutes

Power setting:
FULL

Freezes well

Makes 600ml (1 pint)

To make a darker stock add shoyu, miso or tomato purée.

Illustrated on p. 87

Savoury brown sauce

INGREDIENTS

25g (1 oz) sunflower margarine
2.5ml (½ tsp) celery seeds
1 bay leaf
1 medium onion, finely chopped
1 clove garlic, crushed
25g (1 oz) wholewheat flour
5ml (1 tsp) thyme, chopped fresh
15ml (1 tbsp) shoyu
5-10ml (1-2 tsp) miso
450ml (¾ pint) stock or water
black pepper

This is an easy recipe for a rich gravy which is good served with any savoury bakes or roasts.

1   Put the margarine, celery seeds and bay leaf in a medium dish and ≈ FULL for 1 min. *(30 secs. 700W; 1 min. 500W)*. Stir in the onion and garlic and ≈ FULL for 2 mins. 600W *(1½ mins. 700W; 2½ mins. 500W)*.

2   Stir in the flour and ≈ FULL for 30 secs. Add the chopped thyme and shoyu.

3   Dissolve the miso in a little of the stock or water and mix into the sauce, then add the rest of the stock.

4   Cover and ≈ FULL for 5 mins. 600W *(4 mins. 700W; 6 mins. 500W)*, stirring once or twice. Season with pepper.

★ **Preparation:** 10 minutes

≈ **Cooking time:** 11 minutes

⊘ **Power setting:** FULL

✳ **Freezes well**

◎ **Makes 450ml (¾ pint)**

★ The mixture of shoyu and miso makes a powerful savoury combination, so you can make a well flavoured sauce using only water if you have no stock available.

Illustrated on p. 87

Sweet and sour sauce

INGREDIENTS

15g (½ oz) margarine or butter
½ onion, finely chopped
1 clove garlic, crushed
100ml (4 fl oz) water
100ml (4 fl oz) pineapple juice
15ml (1 tbsp) cider vinegar
10ml (2 tsp) honey
5ml (1 tsp) shoyu
2.5ml (½ tsp) grated fresh root ginger
100g (4 oz) plums, chopped
10ml (2 tsp) arrowroot

Leaving the plums coarsely chopped gives this sauce a good texture. Take care not to over-thicken with arrowroot or the sauce will become gluey.

1   Put the margarine or butter in a medium dish and ≈ FULL for 30 secs. Stir in the onion and garlic and ≈ FULL for 2 mins. 600W *(1½ mins. 700W; 2½ mins. 500W)*.

2   Add the water, fruit juice, vinegar, honey, shoyu, ginger and plums. Cover and ≈ FULL for 5 mins. 600W *(4 mins. 700W; 6 mins. 500W)*, stirring once.

3   Dissolve the arrowroot in a little water, then stir into the sauce and ≈ FULL for 2 mins. 600W *(1½ mins. 700W; 2½ mins. 500W)*, stirring once.

4   Season to taste with salt and pepper.

★ **Preparation:** 15 minutes

≈ **Cooking time:** 9½ minutes

⊘ **Power setting:** FULL

◎ **Makes 300ml (½ pint)**

Illustrated on p. 86

Spiced tomato and coconut sauce

INGREDIENTS

15ml (1 tbsp) sunflower oil
1 onion, finely chopped
1 clove garlic, crushed
1 small red chilli, deseeded and chopped finely
50g (2 oz) creamed coconut
300ml (½ pint) boiling water
3 cloves, ground
2.5ml (½ tsp) ground allspice
30ml (2 tbsp) tomato purée
150ml (¼ pint) tomato juice or equivalent in fresh tomatoes, puréed
salt or shoyu

Creamed coconut makes a marvellous addition to sauces, adding a velvet texture and extra rich flavour. Serve this sauce with nut roasts or bakes, vegetables or polenta.

1   Put the oil in a medium dish and ≈ FULL for 1 min. 600W *(30 secs. 700W; 1 min. 500W)*. Stir in the chopped onion, garlic and chilli and ≈ FULL for 2 mins. 600W *(1½ mins. 700W; 2½ mins. 500W)*.

2   Dissolve the coconut in boiling water, then add to the onion with the remaining ingredients, except the salt or shoyu. Cover and ≈ FULL for 7 mins. 600W *(6 mins. 700W; 8½ mins. 500W)*, stirring once or twice.

3   Season to taste. Liquidize to make a smooth blend.

★ **Preparation:** 10 minutes

≈ **Cooking time:** 10 minutes

⊘ **Power setting:** FULL

≈ **Good reheated**

✳ **Freezes well**

◎ **Makes 600ml (1 pint)**

Illustrated on p. 86

White sauce

Milk-based sauces work particularly well in a microwave as there is little chance of scorching or sticking. Use a container large enough to allow for the liquid's expansion as it heats up. Watch carefully to ensure that it doesn't boil over.

1 Put the milk, onion, bay leaf, peppercorns and herbs in a jug. FULL for 2 mins. 600W *(1½ mins. 700W; 2½ mins. 500W)*. Leave to stand for 5 mins. then strain.

2 Put the margarine or oil in a medium bowl and FULL for 30 secs. Stir in the flour and FULL for 30 secs.

3 Stir in the milk, blending very well. FULL for 2-3 mins. 600W *(1½-2½ mins. 700W; 2½-3½ mins. 500W)* until it coats the back of a spoon, stirring 2-3 times.

INGREDIENTS

300ml (½ pint) milk
½ medium onion
1 bay leaf
6 peppercorns
sprig of parsley or bouquet garni
25g (1 oz) sunflower margarine
25g (1 oz) wholewheat flour
salt and black pepper

★ **Preparation:** 10 minutes

≈ **Cooking time:** 5 minutes

⊘ **Power setting:** FULL

◎ **Makes 300ml (½ pint)**

★ For smooth results, stir milk-based sauces once a minute during cooking. You can even leave a wooden spoon in the mixture while it is in the oven.

Illustrated below

VARIATIONS
Cheese sauce

Make a white sauce following the method above. Once the sauce is cooked, add the cheese and spices. Stir well then cook for 30 secs. or until the cheese is just melted. Do not overcook or the texture will become stringy.

INGREDIENTS

As for white sauce plus
50g (2 oz) grated cheese
pinch of mustard powder or cayenne pepper

◎ **Makes 300ml (½ pint)**

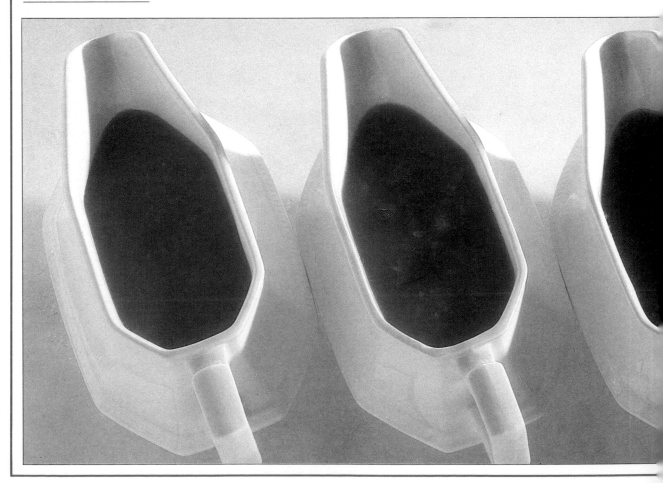

Mushroom sauce

INGREDIENTS

As for white sauce plus

100g (4 oz) button mushrooms, thinly sliced

5ml (1 tsp) paprika

pinch of cayenne pepper

1   Infuse the milk as described opposite, or simply use plain milk and start by heating the margarine.

2   Put the margarine in a medium dish and ≋ FULL for 30 secs. Stir in the mushrooms, spices and seasoning. Cover and ≋ FULL for 4 mins. 600W *(3 mins. 700W; 5 mins. 500W)*, stirring once.

3   Stir in the flour and ≋ FULL for 30 secs.

4   Pour in the milk, stir well, then re-cover. ≋ FULL for 3 mins. 600W *(2½ mins. 700W; 3½ mins. 500W)*, stirring each minute.

◎ **Makes 300ml (½ pint)**

▣ If you don't want to use the sauce immediately, cover the surface with some greaseproof paper to prevent a skin forming.

Carob sauce

INGREDIENTS

25g (1 oz) butter

50g (2 oz) sugar-free carob bar, broken into pieces

1 egg yolk, beaten

250ml (8 fl oz) skimmed milk

This versatile and rich sauce can be used as a topping for steamed puddings, served with poached fruit, such as pears, or raw fruit salads, bananas or ice cream.

1   Put the butter and carob in a medium bowl and ≋ FULL for 2 mins. 600W *(1½ mins. 700W; 2½ mins. 500W)* until melted. Stir well.

2   Beat in the egg yolk and milk and ≋ FULL for 2½ mins. 600W *(2 mins. 700W; 3 mins. 500W)*, stirring 2-3 times. Leave to stand for 2-3 mins. Serve warm.

★ **Preparation:** 5 minutes

≈ **Cooking time:** 4½ minutes

∅ **Power setting:** FULL

◎ **Makes 300ml (½ pint)**

Illustrated on p. 88

From left to right: **Spiced tomato and coconut sauce** *(see p. 85)*; **Sweet and sour sauce** *(see p. 85)*; **Concentrated vegetable stock** *(see p. 84)*; **White sauce** *(see above, left)*, **Savoury brown sauce** *(see p. 85)*

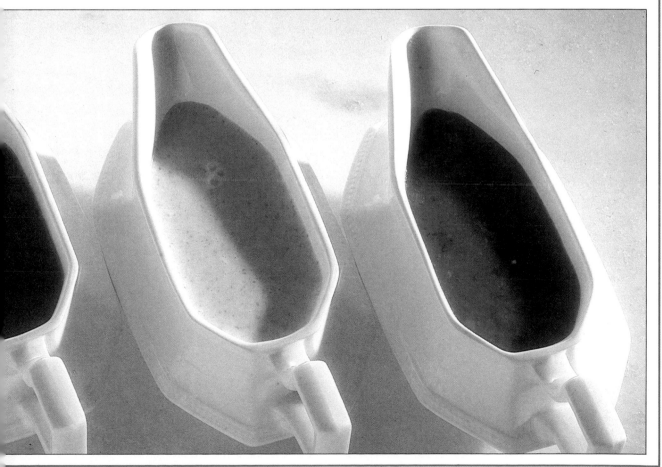

Fruit sauce

INGREDIENTS

50g (2 oz) raisins
150ml (¼ pint) orange juice
1 ripe banana

A refreshing sauce for serving with sponge puddings, baked bananas or ice cream.

1   Put the raisins and orange juice in a jug, cover and ≋ FULL for 2 mins. 600W *(1½ mins. 700W; 2½ mins. 500W)*. Leave for 15-20 mins. until the raisins are plump. Drain, reserving the orange juice.

2   Liquidize the banana with the orange juice until smooth. Add the raisins and liquidize to make a coarse purée.

3   Return the sauce to the jug and ≋ FULL for 2 mins. 600W *(1½ mins. 700W; 2½ mins. 500W)* to reheat. Stir well, then leave to stand for 2-3 mins. before serving.

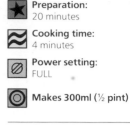

★ **Preparation:** 20 minutes

≋ **Cooking time:** 4 minutes

⊘ **Power setting:** FULL

◎ **Makes 300ml (½ pint)**

Illustrated opposite

Cornmeal custard

INGREDIENTS

300ml (½ pint) skimmed milk or soya milk
45ml (3 tbsp) cornmeal
15-30ml (1-2 tbsp) light brown sugar
2 drops vanilla essence

Custard sauces cook well in the microwave as long as you are careful with the timing and the temperature. Milk can boil over so it is always best to use a large jug or bowl. When not using immediately, cover the surface with greaseproof paper to prevent a skin forming.

1   Put the milk in a jug and ≋ FULL for 1 min. 600W *(30 secs. 700W; 1 min. 500W)*.

2   Mix the cornmeal and sugar together. Beat in a little of the milk to make a smooth paste, then add the remaining milk and the vanilla essence.

3   ≋ FULL for 3½ mins. 600W *(3 mins. 700W; 4-5 mins. 500W)* stirring or whisking 3-4 times during cooking.

★ **Preparation:** 5 minutes

≋ **Cooking time:** 4½ minutes

⊘ **Power setting:** FULL

◎ **Makes 300ml (½ pint)**

 ★ Stir in the cornmeal well so that it doesn't all sink to the bottom in a lump. If this does happen, liquidize the mixture for 30 secs. Whisking with a balloon whisk once a minute during cooking should also ensure smoothness.

Illustrated opposite

Apple and date chutney

INGREDIENTS

225g (8 oz) dessert apples, peeled, cored and chopped
100g (4 oz) onions, chopped
1 clove garlic, crushed
100g (4 oz) dates
75ml (3 fl oz) cider vinegar
100g (4 oz) raisins
1cm (½ in) fresh root ginger, grated
2.5ml (½ tsp) mixed spice
5ml (1 tsp) mustard seeds
pinch of salt
pinch of cayenne pepper

The smell of vinegar and spices doesn't dominate the kitchen when making chutneys and relishes in the microwave, and you can make them in small quantities.

1   Put the apples, onions, garlic, dates and vinegar in a large bowl. Cover and ≋ FULL for 5 mins. 600W *(4 mins. 700W; 6 mins. 500W)*, stirring once.

2   Add the remaining ingredients and ≋ FULL for 12 mins. 600W *(10 mins. 700W; 15 mins. 500W)*, stirring once or twice.

3   Leave to stand overnight, then pour into sterilized jars and store for up to three months.

★ **Preparation:** 20 minutes

≋ **Cooking time:** 17 minutes

⊘ **Power setting:** FULL

◎ **Makes 550g (1¼ lb)**

Illustrated on p. 91

Top: **Fruit sauce** *(see above)*; Centre: **Carob sauce** *(see p. 87)*; Bottom: **Cornmeal custard** *(see above)*

Tomato relish

INGREDIENTS

100g (4 oz) dried apricots, chopped into slivers
60ml (4 tbsp) cider vinegar
225g (8 oz) tomatoes, skinned and chopped
100g (4 oz) medium onion, diced
1 small green pepper, deseeded and chopped
1.25ml (¼ tsp) salt
1 dried chilli, finely chopped
2.5ml (½ tsp) cumin seeds
2.5ml (½ tsp) mustard seeds
2 bay leaves
8 peppercorns

A colourful, spicy relish that complements savoury bakes and nut roasts perfectly.

1   Put the apricots and vinegar in a medium dish and ≊ FULL for 2 mins. 600W *(1½ mins. 700W; 2½ mins. 500W)*. Leave to stand for 30 mins.

2   Mix the remaining ingredients with the apricots. Cover and ≊ FULL for 14 mins. 600W *(11 mins. 700W; 17 mins. 500W)*, stirring several times.

3   Leave to cool then pour into sterilized jars. Store for up to two months.

★ **Preparation:**
15 minutes

≈ **Cooking time:**
16 minutes

⊘ **Power setting:**
FULL

◎ **Makes 550g (1¼ lb)**

★ Prepare clean jars by half-filling with water and bringing to the boil in the microwave. Allow to boil for 1 min. then remove carefully (using oven gloves) and swirl the liquid around each jar before pouring away. Leave jars to dry, turned upside down, on a draining rack or absorbent paper.

Illustrated opposite

Plum and pear jam

INGREDIENTS

450g (1 lb) Victoria plums
1 pear, peeled, cored and chopped
50ml (2 fl oz) concentrated apple juice (CAJ)
15ml (1 tbsp) orange juice
100g (4 oz) soft brown sugar (optional)

This recipe can be used to make a conventional jam or a sugar-free fruit purée, to spread on toast or use as a filling or topping for cakes. Store in the refrigerator, or freeze in small portions.

1   Chop the flesh of the plums coarsely. Mix with the pear, CAJ and orange juice in a large bowl.

2   Crack the plum stones using a rolling pin, and add to the fruit. Count how many are added so that they can all be taken out afterwards.

3   ≊ FULL for 8 mins. 600W *(6½ mins. 700W; 10 mins. 500W)*, stirring once or twice.

4   Leave to cool, remove the stones, then purée. Stir in sugar, if using, and ≊ FULL for 12 mins. 600W *(10 mins. 700W; 15 mins. 500W)*, stirring every 3 mins. Leave to cool then bottle.

★ **Preparation:**
25 minutes

≈ **Cooking time:**
20 minutes

⊘ **Power setting:**
FULL

◎ **Makes 550g (1¼ lb)**

★ For a sugar-free purée, omit the sugar and refrigerate after liquidizing. The purée will thicken in the refrigerator.

Illustrated opposite

Blackberry and apple purée

INGREDIENTS

450g (1 lb) blackberries
225g (8 oz) dessert apples
25ml (1 fl oz) concentrated apple juice
15ml (1 tbsp) lemon juice
Optional
10ml (2 tsp) agar powder

This thick fruit purée can easily be used as a jam, thinly spread on toast or crispbreads, or as a sauce topping. The purée will keep in the refrigerator for about two weeks.

1   Wash all the fruit carefully. Core and chop the apples. Place all the ingredients in a large bowl and ≊ FULL for 8 mins. 600W *(6½ mins. 700W; 10 mins. 500W)*, stirring twice.

2   If you want a thicker consistency, add the agar powder. Dissolve it in the fruit, then ≊ FULL for 2-3 mins. 600W *(1½-2½ mins. 700W; 2½-3½ mins. 500W)*.

3   Leave to cool, then liquidize and sieve to remove the pips. Store in sterilized jars.

★ **Preparation:**
10 minutes

≈ **Cooking time:**
8 minutes

⊘ **Power setting:**
FULL

❄ **Freezes well**

◎ **Makes 450g (1 lb)**

Illustrated opposite

From top to bottom: **Blackberry and apple purée** *(see above)*; **Plum and pear jam** *(see above)*; **Apple and date chutney** *(see p. 88)*; **Tomato relish** *(see above)*

DESSERTS

Fruits, baked cheesecakes and steamed puddings cook particularly well in a microwave. Fresh fruits retain all their colour, flavour and goodness when lightly baked or poached, although you must remember to pierce whole fruits before cooking to stop them bursting. Dried fruits reconstitute quickly and combine well with any fresh fruit in the microwave. Baked egg custards, cereal puddings and fruit sauces all cook successfully, and steamed puddings take minutes rather than hours. Avoid meringue-type desserts as they need large quantities of sugar to microwave successfully. Soufflés, too, are disappointing—they look splendid in the microwave but tend to collapse or to have a rubbery texture.

Millet pudding

INGREDIENTS
25g (1 oz) hazelnuts
50g (2 oz) millet
450ml (¾ pint) concentrated soya milk
50g (2 oz) dried apricots, cut into slivers
50g (2 oz) raisins
25g (1 oz) demerara sugar
2.5ml (½ tsp) allspice
1.25ml (¼ tsp) grated nutmeg
To serve
60ml (4 tbsp) concentrated soya milk

Traditional milk puddings, especially rice, really do need the slow cooking of a conventional oven. However, millet is such a creamy grain that this recipe works well in a microwave, especially when using a concentrated soya milk. Any leftovers can be reheated to make a special breakfast cereal.

1　Spread out the hazelnuts on a small plate and ≋ FULL for 3 mins. 600W *(2½ mins. 700W; 3½ mins. 500W),* shaking the plate halfway through. Put the nuts in a clean cloth and rub off the skins. Chop the nuts finely and reserve 15ml (1 tbsp) for decorating the pudding .

2　Mix all the other ingredients together in a large dish, adding 150ml (¼ pint) water to dilute the concentrated soya milk.

3　Cover and ≋ FULL for 5 mins. 600W *(4 mins. 700W; 6 mins. 500W),* stirring twice, then ≋ MEDIUM-HIGH for 12 mins, 600W *(10 mins. 700W; ≋ FULL for 10-12 mins. 500W),* stirring every 3 mins. Leave to stand for 10 mins. after cooking.

4　Decorate with the chopped nuts and serve with concentrated soya milk.

 Preparation:
10 minutes

Cooking time:
25 minutes

 **Power settings:**
FULL and MEDIUM-HIGH

 Serves 4

If you can't get hold of concentrated soya milk, use 500ml (17 fl oz) ordinary soya milk, which doesn't need diluting with water.

Illustrated on p. 94

Carob pudding

INGREDIENTS

100g (4 oz) margarine or butter
100g (4 oz) barbados sugar
2 eggs
100g (4 oz) wholewheat flour
30ml (2 tbsp) carob powder
10ml (2 tsp) baking powder
15-30ml (1-2 tbsp) yogurt

This rich, dark pudding is quick to microwave and the end result is light with a crumbly, spongy texture. Serve with yogurt and honey mixed together, a purée of dried or fresh fruit, or a cornmeal custard.

1 Cream the margarine and sugar together in a medium dish until light and fluffy. ≈ FULL for 5 secs.

2 Beat in the eggs one at a time, then fold in the flour, carob and baking powder.

3 Add enough yogurt to give the mixture a soft, dropping consistency.

4 Line a 1.2 litre (2 pint) pudding basin with greaseproof paper, then spoon in the pudding mixture. Cover and ≈ FULL for 5-6 mins. 600W *(4-5 mins. 700W; 6-7½ mins. 500W)*, giving the dish a quarter turn every 1½ mins.

5 Leave to stand for 5 mins. before serving.

Preparation:
10 minutes

Cooking time:
5-6 minutes

Power setting:
FULL

Serves 4

Once the mixture is made up it should be cooked straight away to get the full benefit of the baking powder.

Illustrated on p. 94

Baked pears with mango sauce

INGREDIENTS

4 large pears
300ml (½ pint) orange juice
juice of ½ lemon
2.5cm (1 in) fresh root ginger, cut into slivers
1 mango, peeled and diced
10ml (2 tsp) arrowroot

A delicious, light dessert with an interesting combination of fruits. Use ripe William or Packham pears and choose a ripe mango by its distinctive scent.

1 Peel the pears, halve and core them. Arrange around the outside of a large round dish, cut side down, with the thicker ends pointing outwards.

2 Pour over the orange and lemon juice and add the ginger. Cover and ≈ FULL for 5 mins. 600W *(4 mins. 700W; 6 mins. 500W)*, giving the dish a quarter turn every 1½ mins.

3 Strain off the excess juice, then liquidize the mango in the fruit juice until smooth.

4 Dissolve the arrowroot in a little of the fruit juice, then stir into the remainder.

5 Pour into a jug and ≈ FULL for 4 mins. 600W *(3 mins. 700W; 5 mins. 500W)*, stirring once every minute until the sauce has boiled and thickened.

6 Pour the sauce over the pears and ≈ FULL for 1 min. to reheat if necessary.

Preparation:
15 minutes

Cooking time:
9 minutes

Power setting:
FULL

Serves 4

Illustrated on p. 94

Plum and banana crumble

INGREDIENTS

450g (1 lb) plums, stoned and chopped
2 bananas, sliced
30ml (2 tbsp) concentrated apple juice
For the topping
50g (2 oz) wholewheat flour
50g (2 oz) coarse oatmeal
50g (2 oz) sunflower margarine
25g (1 oz) sunflower seeds
30ml (2 tbsp) demerara sugar

Choose mixtures of dried and fresh fruits for natural sweetness and a better flavour: try fig and rhubarb, or cooking apples with dates or raisins.

1 Mix the plums and bananas with the concentrated apple juice in a medium dish. Cover and ≋ FULL for 4 mins. 600W *(3 mins. 700W; 5 mins. 500W)*.

2 For the topping, mix the flour and oatmeal together. Rub in the margarine, then stir in the seeds and sugar.

3 Sprinkle the crumble topping over the fruit, then ≋ FULL for 3 mins. 600W *(2½ mins. 700W; 3½ mins. 500W)*, giving the dish a quarter turn every minute.

4 Serve hot or warm.

★ **Preparation:** 15 minutes

≋ **Cooking time:** 7 minutes

∅ **Power setting:** FULL

◎ **Serves 4**

★ The crumble topping needs to be made with quite coarse ingredients, and some sugar, to get a good texture. Oatmeal is ideal, so too are small seeds such as sunflower or sesame.

Illustrated on p. 97

Apricot petit pots

INGREDIENTS

100g (4 oz) dried apricots
600ml (1 pint) boiling water
2 eggs
15g (½ oz) flaked almonds, chopped
25g (1 oz) cornmeal
150ml (¼ pint) skimmed milk
2.5ml (¼ tsp) ground cardamom
15-30ml (1-2 tbsp) honey (optional)

Egg custards and cornmeal custards work extremely well in the microwave and can be flavoured with different fruit purées or a variety of spices and sweeteners.

1 Cover the apricots with boiling water. Cover and ≋ FULL for 5 mins. 600W *(4 mins. 700W; 6 mins. 500W)*. Leave until cool and plump. Drain, then purée.

2 Arrange the almonds on a small plate and toast on ≋ FULL for about 3 mins. 600W *(2 mins. 700W; 4 mins. 500W)*, stirring at least once a minute to prevent scorching.

3 Whisk together the remaining ingredients, sweetening to taste with honey if wished. Mix in the apricot purée.

4 Divide the mixture between four ramekin dishes. ≋ FULL 5 mins. 600W *(4 mins. 700W; 6 mins. 500W)*, rearranging the dishes halfway through.

5 Decorate with the flaked almonds.

★ **Preparation:** 15 minutes, plus cooling

≋ **Cooking time:** 10 minutes

∅ **Power setting:** FULL

◎ **Serves 4**

Illustrated on p. 97

Top right: **Carob pudding** *(see p. 93)*; Centre left: **Millet pudding** *(see p. 92)*; Bottom: **Baked pears with mango sauce** *(see p. 93)*

Summer compote

INGREDIENTS

225g (8 oz) blackcurrants
225g (8 oz) redcurrants
10ml (2 tsp) arrowroot
15ml (1 tbsp) concentrated apple juice (CAJ)
30ml (2 tbsp) honey

This refreshing pudding is simple to make in the microwave, and the cooking method preserves the texture of the individual berries. Other combinations of summer fruits can be used such as white currants, blackberries and raspberries.

1 String the currants, then liquidize or mash half of them.

2 Dissolve the arrowroot in the CAJ mixed with 25ml (1 fl oz) water. Add the honey and stir into the fruit purée.

3 Spoon into a medium dish, cover and ≈ FULL for 4 mins. 600W *(3 mins. 700W; 5 mins. 500W)*, stirring once or twice.

4 Add the remaining fruit and ≈ FULL for 1 min. 600W *(30 secs. 700W; 1 min. 500W)*.

5 Serve chilled accompanied by yogurt or sour cream.

Preparation:
15 minutes, plus chilling

Cooking time:
5 minutes

Power setting:
FULL

Serves 4

Illustrated below

From left to right: **Summer compote** *(see above)*; **Apricot petit pots** *(see p. 95)*; **Plum and banana crumble** *(see p. 95)*

Mixed fruit compote

INGREDIENTS

350g (12 oz) mixed dried fruit (prunes, peaches, apple rings, apricots, figs)
25g (1 oz) raisins
300ml (½ pint) red wine or red grape juice
6 cardamom pods
6 cloves
5cm (2 in) piece cinnamon stick
honey, to sweeten
flaked almonds, to decorate

Dried fruits are a good standby to have in the store-cupboard, and with the microwave they come into their own for making emergency puddings or an instant breakfast.

1   Put all the ingredients, except the honey and almonds, in a large bowl, and add 150ml (¼ pint) warm water. Cover and ≋ FULL for 10 mins. 600W *(8½ mins. 700W; 12½ mins. 500W)*, stirring once or twice.

2   Leave to stand for 10-30 mins. then sweeten to taste with honey if necessary. Discard the whole spices.

3   ≋ FULL for 1 min. 600W *(30 secs. 700W; 1 min. 500W)* to reheat, then spoon into individual dishes.

4   Sprinkle flaked almonds over the top and serve warm.

★ **Preparation:**
15-35 minutes

≋ **Cooking time:**
11 minutes

⊘ **Power setting:**
FULL

▤ **Make in advance**

◎ **Serves 4**

★ Try other spices, such as allspice or coriander, and different varieties of fruit juice— orange is especially good for flavour.

Illustrated on p. 99

Christmas pudding

INGREDIENTS

75g (3 oz) wholewheat flour
5ml (1 tsp) mixed spice
5ml (1 tsp) ground cinnamon
2.5ml (½ tsp) grated nutmeg
finely grated rind and juice of ½ lemon
50g (2 oz) creamed coconut, grated
75g (3 oz) wholewheat breadcrumbs
50g (2 oz) muscovado sugar
100g (4 oz) carrots, grated
1 dessert apple, grated
100g (4 oz) raisins
100g (4 oz) currants
100g (4 oz) sultanas
50g (2 oz) dates
30ml (2 tbsp) molasses
2 eggs
45ml (3 tbsp) brandy
15ml (1 tbsp) carob powder (optional)

Microwaving this type of pudding is a great time saver. As the flavours have less time to develop during cooking, the raw mixture should be left to stand overnight.

1   Mix all the ingredients together in a large bowl, adding the carob powder if a darker colour is preferred. The mixture should be moist enough to drop off the spoon—add more brandy or fruit juice if necessary.

2   Cover the bowl with cling film and chill for several hours or overnight so the flavours can combine.

3   Grease a 1.2 litre (2 pint) basin. Spoon in the mixture, cover and ≋ FULL for 5 mins. 600W *(4 mins. 700W; 6 mins. 500W)*, then let it stand for 5 mins. Repeat this process 3 times to cook the pudding thoroughly.

4   If you are not serving the pudding immediately, store in a cool place wrapped in foil or cling film. Unwrap when required and cook, covered, in a basin. Reheat for 5 mins. and stand for 5 mins. before serving.

★ **Preparation:**
15 minutes, plus standing

≋ **Cooking time:**
20 minutes, plus standing

⊘ **Power setting:**
FULL

▤ **Make in advance**

◎ **Serves 8**

★ Remember not to put metal trinkets in the pudding when you cook or reheat it in the microwave.

Illustrated opposite

Chestnut cheesecake

INGREDIENTS

100g (4 oz) dried chestnuts
600ml (1 pint) boiling water
50g (2 oz) sunflower margarine
25g (1 oz) soft brown sugar
50g (2 oz) oatflakes
For the topping
150ml (¼ pint) skimmed milk
2 eggs, separated
45ml (3 tbsp) honey
400g (14 oz) quark
5ml (1 tsp) finely grated orange rind
5ml (1 tsp) grated fresh root ginger
2.5ml (½ tsp) vanilla essence
stem ginger and fresh orange slices, to decorate

The finished cheesecake is quite delicate, so handle it carefully. You may need to cook it a little longer than recommended here for a firmer texture but be careful not to dry out the mixture as it will continue setting as it cools.

1   Put the chestnuts in a deep dish, pour over the boiling water and leave to soak for 1 hour. Cover and ≋ FULL for 5 mins. 600W *(4 mins. 700W; 6 mins. 500W)* until boiling, then ≋ MEDIUM for 15 mins. 600W *(12½ mins. 700W; ≋ DEFROST for 22 mins. 500W)*. Drain and grind.

2   Cream the margarine and sugar together. Add the chestnuts and oatflakes. Mix to a dough. Press into a 20cm (8 in) flan dish and ≋ FULL for 4 mins. 600W *(3 mins. 700W; 5 mins. 500W)* giving the dish a quarter turn every minute.

3   For the topping, put the milk in a jug and ≋ FULL for 1 min. 600W *(30 secs. 700W; 1 min. 500W)*. Beat in the egg yolks and 15ml (1 tbsp) honey and ≋ MEDIUM for 2-5 mins. 600W *(1½-4 mins. 700W; ≋ DEFROST for 5-9 mins. 500W)*, stirring once every half minute until the mixture thickens. If the custard starts cooking too quickly, reduce the control setting to LOW and continue cooking until the custard thickens.

4   Whisk the egg whites until stiff. Beat the remaining ingredients into the custard, then fold in the egg whites. Pour on top of the base, then ≋ FULL for 5-6 mins. 600W *(4-5 mins. 700W; 6-7 mins. 500W)*. Cool thoroughly. Decorate with stem ginger and orange slices. Serve chilled.

★ **Preparation:**
15 minutes, plus 1 hour soaking

≋ **Cooking time:**
32 minutes

⊘ **Power setting:**
FULL and MEDIUM

◎ **Serves 4**

★ Dried chestnuts add extra flavour to the base, and are easy to reconstitute in a microwave either by the soaking method given here or from dried (see p. 23).

Illustrated on p. 101

Top: **Christmas pudding** *(see above)* Bottom: **Mixed fruit compote** *(see p. 97)*

Stuffed peaches in wine sauce

INGREDIENTS

4 peaches
175g (6 oz) cherries, stoned
25g (1 oz) chopped nuts
300ml (½ pint) rosé wine or apple juice
15ml (1 tbsp) arrowroot
2.5ml (½ tsp) ground cinnamon

It's easy to heat fruit through without losing its colour or texture, to make a distinctive and appetizing dish. Here the peach halves are filled with cherries and nuts and topped with a light wine or fruit-based sauce.

1   Slice the peaches in half, stone and arrange skin-side down around the edge of a large round dish.

2   Chop the cherries very finely, mix with the chopped nuts and spoon this mixture on top of each peach.

3   Pour over the wine or apple juice, cover and ≋ FULL for 4 mins. 600W *(3 mins. 700W; 5 mins. 500W)*, rearranging halfway through the cooking time.

4   Strain off the juice into a jug. Mix the arrowroot with a little of this juice, then stir it back in to the remainder. Add the cinnamon and ≋ FULL for 3 mins. 600W *(2½ mins. 700W; 3½ mins. 500W)*, stirring once or twice.

5   Pour the sauce over the peaches and ≋ FULL for 1 min.

6   Serve hot or chilled, with yogurt, smetana or ice-cream.

★ **Preparation:**
10 minutes

≋ **Cooking time:**
8 minutes

⊘ **Power setting:**
FULL

◎ **Serves 4**

★ Other soft summer fruits such as raspberries, redcurrants or blackcurrants could be used in the filling instead of the cherries.

Illustrated opposite

Carob and raisin chiffon pie

INGREDIENTS

50g (2 oz) sunflower margarine
15ml (1 tbsp) pear and apple spread
50g (2 oz) oat flakes
50g (2 oz) wholewheat flour
For the topping
100g (4 oz) raisins
150ml (¼ pint) apple juice or water
300g (11 oz) silken tofu
30-45ml (2-3 tbsp) concentrated apple juice (CAJ)
15ml (1 tbsp) brandy
10ml (2 tsp) carob powder

Plumping raisins in fruit juice—so easily done in the microwave—and then puréeing them results in a wonderful sweet sauce with a good dark colour and slightly rough texture. Combined with silken tofu, this makes a light but flavoursome topping.

1   Cream the margarine and the pear and apple spread until smooth and light. Add the oats and flour and mix well.

2   Spread the mixture in a 20cm (8 in) round dish and cover with greaseproof paper and a plate. ≋ FULL for 4 mins. 600W *(3 mins. 700W; 5 mins. 500W)*. Uncover and leave to cool.

3   For the topping, put the raisins in a medium dish and pour over the apple juice or water. ≋ FULL for 2 mins. 600W *(1½ mins. 700W; 2½ mins. 500W)*. Leave to stand for 15 mins., then drain and liquidize to make a textured purée.

4   Liquidize the tofu, CAJ, brandy and carob powder until smooth. Stir in the raisins. Pour the topping over the base ≋ MEDIUM-HIGH for 6 mins. 600W *(5 mins. 700W; ≋ FULL for 5 mins. 500W)*, then ≋ MEDIUM for 2 mins. 600W *(1½ mins. 700W; ≋ DEFROST for 3 mins. 500W)*.

5   Leave to cool, then chill before serving.

6   Decorate with grated carob chocolate if desired.

★ **Preparation:**
25 minutes, plus chilling

≋ **Cooking time:**
14 minutes

⊘ **Power settings:**
FULL, MEDIUM-HIGH and MEDIUM

◎ **Serves 4**

Illustrated opposite

Top left: **Carob and raisin chiffon pie** *(see above)*; Top right: **Chestnut cheesecake** *(see p. 98)*; Bottom: **Stuffed peaches in wine sauce** *(see above)*

BREADS, CAKES AND BISCUITS

Baked products can work well in the microwave but you must allow for the fact that the results will not have the golden brown or crisp finish achieved by conventional baking. Using wholewheat flour gives a more appetizing, pale brown colour to all baked products and you can add carob, dark spices or molasses to cake and biscuit mixtures to improve their appearance further. Bread cooks successfully by microwave producing light, moist loaves. I think it's essential, however, to rise and prove the dough in the ordinary way. Although the microwave speeds up this process dramatically, there is no chance for the flavours to develop. But once the dough has proved, bread-baking takes only a few minutes in the microwave. Most cakes bake well, provided the initial mixture is moist and you do not overfill the container. Add some dark ingredients to improve the colour of the mixture or decorate the finished cake with toasted chopped nuts, fresh fruit or a light topping if you think it looks unappetizing. Biscuits are, in my experience, the least successful items to microwave. Crisp biscuits are best cooked conventionally but moister mixtures, like flapjacks, which are cooked on a tray and then cut into slices, can work in the microwave.

Soda bread

INGREDIENTS

450g (1 lb) wholewheat flour
2.5ml (½ tsp) salt
5ml (1 tsp) bicarbonate of soda
50g (2 oz) butter
225ml (8 fl oz) buttermilk
extra liquid for mixing

This type of dough works extremely well in the microwave. It is important to bake the mixture straight away, otherwise the effect of the soda is lost.

1 Mix the flour, salt and bicarbonate of soda together, then rub in the butter. Add the buttermilk and mix to a stiff dough.

2 Knead the dough into a cob shape. Place on a small plate or flat dish and make a deep cross on the top.

3 ≈ FULL for 7 mins. 600W *(6 mins. 700W; 8½ mins. 500W)*, giving the plate or dish a half turn every 2-3 mins.

4 Leave to stand and cool on a wire rack.

★ **Preparation:**
15 minutes, plus cooling

 Cooking time:
7 minutes

 Power setting:
FULL

◎ **Makes a 700g (1½ lb) loaf**

★ Remember never to put the dough into traditional metal loaf tins, use bakeware specially designed for use in microwave ovens.

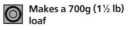

Illustrated on p. 104

Wholewheat bread

INGREDIENTS

700g (1½ lb) wholewheat flour
5ml (1 tsp) salt
25g (1 oz) fresh yeast
15ml (1 tbsp) molasses
450ml (¾ pint) tepid water
30ml (2 tbsp) soya flour

A microwave oven makes the actual baking of bread a very speedy process. You can also prove dough in the microwave oven, but the flavour is not as good, the timing is tricky and if you are not careful you end up with a half-cooked, half-risen loaf!

1   Mix the flour and salt together in a large bowl. Cream the yeast and molasses together. Add 150ml (¼ pint) water and whisk until the yeast is dissolved. Add the soya flour, then leave the mixture in a warm place for 5 mins.

2   Pour the yeast ferment into the flour and add the remaining water. Knead well to form a smooth, pliable dough. It should not be dry at this stage. Place in a clean bowl, cover with cling film and leave to rise for at least 15-30 mins.

3   Knead again briefly, then divide the dough in two. Shape each piece into a loaf and put in a 450g (1 lb) loaf dish. Cover with cling film and leave to prove to 30 mins. Prick well.

4   Uncover and bake one loaf at a time. ≋ FULL for 7 mins. 600W *(6 mins. 700W; 8½ mins. 500W)*, giving the dish a half turn every 2-3 mins.

5   Leave to stand in the dish, then turn on to a wire rack and leave to cool. Don't be tempted to eat the bread hot from the oven. It needs to stand and cool to finish cooking.

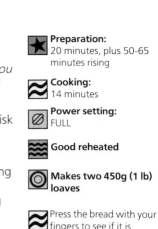

Preparation:
20 minutes, plus 50-65 minutes rising

Cooking:
14 minutes

Power setting:
FULL

Good reheated

Makes two 450g (1 lb) loaves

Press the bread with your fingers to see if it is ready—it should spring back when it is. Do not overcook in the oven as the bread continues to cook through during the standing time.

Illustrated on p. 105

Mixed seed loaf

INGREDIENTS

15ml (1 tbsp) pumpkin seeds
15ml (1 tbsp) sunflower seeds
15ml (1 tbsp) sesame seeds
15ml (1 tbsp) linseeds
15ml (1 tbsp) poppy seeds
1 quantity of wholewheat bread dough (see above)

A nutty loaf which has an interesting texture. Its flavour is heightened by the seeds being toasted first. Vary the seed mixture according to what you have available: the overall quantity should be about 50g (2 oz).

1   Put the seeds in a shallow dish and ≋ FULL for 2 mins. 600W *(1½ mins. 700W; 2½ mins. 500W)* stirring or shaking several times to prevent any scorching.

2   Make the dough according to the instructions for Wholewheat bread, above, adding the seeds to the flour and salt mixture. The addition of soya flour is optional in this recipe.

Preparation:
20 minutes, plus 50-65 minutes rising

Cooking time:
16 minutes

Power setting:
FULL

Makes two 450g (1 lb) loaves

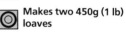
You can improve the appearance of loaves by topping with toasted buckwheat, sesame seeds or poppy seeds.

Illustrated on p. 104

Cheese and oat cob

This makes a tasty, pleasantly chewy savoury bread which is delicious served with soups or mixed vegetable dishes.

INGREDIENTS

25g (1 oz) fresh yeast
15ml (1 tbsp) molasses
300-450ml (½-¾ pint) tepid water
450g (1 lb) wholewheat flour
225g (8 oz) oat flakes
50g (2 oz) Cheddar cheese, grated
5ml (1 tsp) salt
5ml (1 tsp) paprika
5ml (1 tsp) caraway seeds

1 Mix the yeast with the molasses and 300ml (½ pint) tepid water. Leave for 5 mins.

2 Stir in half the wholewheat flour and ≋ FULL for 1 min. 600W *(30 secs. 700W; 1 min. 500W)*, stirring halfway through.

3 Add the remaining ingredients and knead well, adding a little more water if necessary. Cover with cling film and leave to rise for about 30 mins.

4 Knead again, then divide the dough into two. Shape into cobs or shape each half into five rolls. Cover with cling film and leave to prove for 1 hour.

5 Uncover and bake cobs one at a time on a small plate or flat dish. ≋ FULL for 7 mins. 600W *(6 mins. 700W; 8½ mins. 500W)*, giving the plate or dish a half turn every 2-3 mins. Bake rolls in two batches, arrange in a ring on a dish and ≋ FULL for 4 mins. 600W *(3 mins. 700W; 5 mins. 500W)*, giving the dish a half turn halfway through. Leave to cool on a wire rack.

★ **Preparation:**
25 minutes, plus 1½ hours rising and proving

≋ **Cooking time:**
15 minutes

⊘ **Power setting:**
FULL

◎ **Makes 2 cobs or 10 rolls**

★ The microwave is extremely useful for speeding up the action of the yeast when making bread by the batter method. The batter quickly becomes light and frothy.

Illustrated opposite

From left to right: **Soda bread** *(see p. 102);* **Mixed seed loaf** *(see p. 103);* **Wholewheat bread** *(see p. 103);* **Cheese and oat cob** *(see above)*

Savoury scone roll

This is a useful recipe for a quick snack at home, or for picnics and packed lunches. The filling can be varied by using different nuts and adding extra herbs and vegetables, but be sure that they are all finely chopped.

INGREDIENTS

225g (8 oz) self-raising wholewheat flour
pinch of salt
5ml (1 tsp) baking powder
pinch of cayenne pepper
50g (2 oz) margarine
1 egg, beaten
45-60ml (3-4 tbsp) milk
For the filling
15ml (1 tbsp) sunflower oil
1 medium onion, finely chopped
1 clove garlic, crushed
15ml (1 tbsp) chutney
15ml (1 tbsp) tomato purée
100g (4 oz) walnuts, chopped
salt and black pepper

1   For the filling, put the oil in a medium dish and ≋ FULL for 1 min. 600W *(30 secs. 700W; 1 min. 500W).* Stir in the chopped onion and garlic and ≋ FULL for 1 min. 600W *(30 secs. 700W; 1 min. 500W).*

2   Stir in the remaining ingredients for the filling, except the seasoning, and ≋ FULL for 2 mins *(1½ mins. 700W; 2½ mins. 500W).* Season well.

3   For the scone, mix the flour, salt, baking powder and cayenne together. Rub in the fat, then add the beaten egg and enough milk to make a soft dough.

4   Roll out the dough to a 22.5 x 15cm (9 x 6 in) rectangle. Spread over the filling, then roll up the dough from long edge to long edge.

5   Wrap in greaseproof paper and place in a flat dish. ≋ FULL for 4½ mins. 600W *(3½-4 mins. 700W; 5½-6 mins. 500W)* giving the dish a half turn every 2 mins. Serve hot or cold.

★ **Preparation:** 20 minutes

≈ **Cooking time:** 8½ minutes

⊘ **Power setting:** FULL

❋ **Freezes well**

◎ **Serves 4**

★ Wrapping the roll in greaseproof paper helps retain the moisture and keep the dough soft.

Illustrated on p. 107

Honey and sesame scones

INGREDIENTS

225g (8 oz) self-raising wholewheat flour
pinch of salt
5ml (1 tsp) baking powder
5ml (1 tsp) mixed spice
50g (2 oz) sunflower margarine
25g (1 oz) sesame seeds
30ml (2 tbsp) honey
1 egg, beaten
30-45ml (2-3 tbsp) milk

Scone dough microwaves well and using wholewheat flour gives the scones a good colour. The sesame seeds provide a delicious crunchy quality and the honey adds just enough sweetness.

1 Mix the flour, salt, baking powder and mixed spice together. Rub in the fat, then mix in the sesame seeds.

2 Add the honey, beaten egg and enough milk to make a soft, pliable dough.

3 Quickly pat out the dough to a large round and mark into eight sections. Place on a dish lined with greaseproof paper and ≋ FULL for 4 mins. 600W *(3 mins. 700W; 5 mins. 500W)*, giving the dish a half turn every 2 mins. Leave to stand for 4 mins. Eat warm.

★ **Preparation:** 15 minutes

≋ **Cooking time:** 4 minutes

⊘ **Power setting:** FULL

❄ **Freezes well**

◎ **Serves 8**

Illustrated opposite

Orange cake

INGREDIENTS

1 orange
15ml (1 tbsp) concentrated apple juice
100g (4 oz) sugar
100ml (4 fl oz) sunflower oil
225g (8 oz) wholewheat flour
5ml (1 tsp) mixed spice
5ml (1 tsp) baking powder
pinch of salt
For the decoration
fresh orange slices
desiccated coconut

This simple cake has a good texture and delicious flavour. The cake can be made with lemon if preferred.

1 Scrub the orange well, and chop into small pieces. Liquidize with 200ml (7 fl oz) water and the concentrated apple juice until fairly smooth. Add the sugar and oil and liquidize again.

2 Mix the flour with the spice, salt and baking powder. Stir in the orange mixture until smooth.

3 Line a 1.2 litre (2 pint) ring mould or savarin dish with greaseproof paper. Spoon in the cake mixture and ≋ FULL for 8 mins. 600W *(6½ mins. 700W; 10 mins. 500W)*, giving the dish a quarter turn every 2 mins.

4 Leave to stand for 5-10 mins. before turning out on a wire rack to cool. Remove the paper at the end of the standing time to prevent it sticking to the cake.

5 Decorate with orange slices or desiccated coconut.

★ **Preparation:** 10 minutes

≋ **Cooking time:** 8 minutes

⊘ **Power setting:** FULL

❄ **Freezes well**

◎ **Serves 8**

★ At the end of the cooking time most cakes still look damp on top. Leave to stand for the time specified, then insert a skewer into the centre. If the skewer comes out clean the cake is cooked; if not, cook the cake for a further 1-2 mins, then leave to stand again.

Illustrated opposite

Top: **Savoury scone roll** *(see 105)*; Bottom right: **Honey and sesame scone** *(see above)*; Left: **Orange cake** *(see above)*

Fruit tea bread

INGREDIENTS

100g (4 oz) raisins
150ml (¼ pint) apple or orange juice
225-300ml (8-10 fl oz) skimmed milk
20g (¾ oz) fresh yeast
25g (1 oz) muscovado sugar
50g (2 oz) margarine or butter
2 eggs
450g (1 lb) wholewheat flour
pinch of salt
2.5ml (½ tsp) ground cinnamon

Microwaving this enriched dough produces a light, airy texture. It is important that the dough proves in the normal way so that the flavours develop well.

1 Put the raisins and apple or orange juice in a small bowl, cover and ≋ FULL for 2 mins. 600W *(1½ mins. 700W; 2½ mins. 500W)*. Leave to cool.

2 Put the milk in a jug and ≋ FULL for 2 mins. 600W *(1½ mins. 700W; 2½ mins. 500W)* until quite warm.

3 Cream the yeast and sugar together, then add 150ml (¼ pint) milk. Whisk well, then leave for 5 mins.

4 Put the margarine in a medium dish and ≋ FULL for 30-60 secs. until melted. Stir into the yeast mixture, then beat in the eggs. Add the flour, salt and cinnamon and the remaining milk—the dough should be soft but not sticky. Knead well.

5 Drain the raisins and work into the dough. Place in a clean bowl, cover with a cloth and leave for at least 1 hour.

6 Knock back, knead again, then place in a greased 1.4 litre (2½ pint) or 1Kg (2 lb) dish. Cover and leave for 1 hour.

7 ≋ FULL for 11 mins. 600W *(9 mins. 700W; 13½ mins. 500W)*, giving the dish a quarter turn every 2 mins. Leave to stand for 5-10 mins. then turn out onto a wire rack to cool.

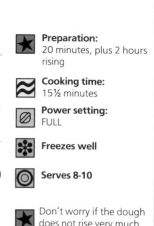

★ **Preparation:**
20 minutes, plus 2 hours rising

≋ **Cooking time:**
15½ minutes

⊘ **Power setting:**
FULL

❄ **Freezes well**

◎ **Serves 8-10**

★ Don't worry if the dough does not rise very much during proving—it soon rises in the microwave.

Illustrated opposite

Parkin

INGREDIENTS

100g (4 oz) dried apricots, diced
175ml (6 fl oz) boiling water
225g (8 oz) wholewheat flour
225g (8 oz) oatmeal
salt
2.5ml (½ tsp) bicarbonate of soda
2.5ml (½ tsp) baking powder
15ml (1 tbsp) ground ginger
100g (4 oz) sunflower margarine
150ml (¼ pint) molasses
50ml (2 fl oz) honey
2 eggs

The strong flavour and colour of this delicious traditional cake make it ideal for microwave cookery. Coarse oatmeal gives a rough texture to the cake; use fine oatmeal or oatflakes for a less chewy finish.

1 Put the apricots in a bowl and pour over the boiling water. Cover and ≋ FULL for 5 mins. 600W *(4 mins. 700W; 6 mins. 500W)*. Liquidize until smooth.

2 Mix the flour, oatmeal, salt, bicarbonate of soda, baking powder and ginger together in a large bowl.

3 Put the margarine in a medium dish and ≋ FULL for 1 min. 600W *(30 secs. 700W; 1 min. 500W)*. Add the molasses and honey and ≋ FULL for 1 min. 600W *(30 secs. 700W; 1 min. 500W)*. Stir well.

4 Pour the melted molasses and honey mixture into the dry ingredients, stirring well. Add the apricot purée and the beaten eggs. Mix together well.

5 Line a 22.5 x 17.5cm (9 x 7 in) rectangular dish with greaseproof paper. Spoon in the mixture and ≋ FULL for 8 mins. 600W *(6½ mins. 700W; 10½ mins. 500W)*, giving the dish a quarter turn every 2 mins. Leave to stand for 10 mins. then turn out onto a wire rack to cool. Remove the paper at the end of the standing time to prevent it sticking to the parkin.

★ **Preparation:**
20 minutes

≋ **Cooking time:**
13 minutes

⊘ **Power setting:**
FULL

❄ **Freezes well**

◎ **Serves 9**

≋ Watch the corner areas when using rectangular dishes in the microwave as they tend to overcook. You can shield them with triangles of foil toward the end of the cooking time.

Illustrated opposite

Top left: **Fruit tea bread** *(see above)*; Top right: **Parkin** *(see above)*; Bottom: **Carrot and sultana cake** *(see p. 110)*

Carrot and sultana cake

INGREDIENTS

100g (4 oz) sultanas
150ml (¼ pint) orange juice
2 eggs
100g (4 oz) sugar
175ml (6 fl oz) sunflower oil
225g (8 oz) carrots, grated
225g (8 oz) wholewheat flour
10ml (2 tsp) ground cinnamon
2.25ml (½ tsp) grated nutmeg
5ml (1 tsp) baking powder
pinch of salt
For the decoration
a little warm jam
chopped nuts

To ensure even cooking with large cakes it is a good idea to use a ring dish, such as a savarin dish. The carrots and orange juice give this cake a golden colour, and the sultana purée is a good substitute for sugar.

1   Put the sultanas and orange juice in a small dish and ≈ FULL for 2 mins. 600W *(1½ mins. 700W; 2½ mins. 500W)*.

2   Leave to stand for 20 mins. then liquidize until smooth. Beat in the eggs, then add the sugar and oil and mix well. Stir in the grated carrot.

3   Mix the flour, spices, baking powder and salt together then stir into the other ingredients.

4   Line a savarin dish with greaseproof paper. Spoon in the mixture and ≈ FULL for 8 mins. 600W *(6½ mins. 700W; 10 mins. 500W)*, giving the dish a quarter turn every 2-3 mins.

5   Leave to stand for 3-4 mins. then turn out onto a wire rack to cool. Remove the paper at the end of the standing time to prevent it sticking to the cake.

6   Spread with a little warm jam and decorate with chopped nuts before serving.

★ **Preparation:**
30 minutes, plus cooling

≈ **Cooking time:**
10 minutes

⊘ **Power setting:**
FULL

❋ **Freezes well**

◎ **Serves 8-10**

★ If a savarin dish is not available, use a deep flan dish with an inverted bowl in the centre. If freezing the cake, freeze it undecorated.

Illustrated on p. 108

Date and carob slice

INGREDIENTS

100g (4 oz) dried dates, chopped
150ml (¼ pint) boiling water
100g (4 oz) sunflower margarine
1 banana mashed
100g (4 oz) wholewheat flour
50g (2 oz) soya flour
50g (2 oz) carob powder
pinch of salt
5ml (1 tsp) baking powder
50ml (2 fl oz) orange juice
50g (2 oz) blanched, chopped nuts

Cake mixtures with carob work well in a microwave because of its dark colour. The texture of this slice is rather like fudge, and is best when left to cool completely.

1   Put the dates in a small dish and pour over the boiling water. Cover and ≈ FULL for 3 mins. 600W *(2½ mins. 700W; 3½ mins. 500W)*. Cool thoroughly, then beat to a smooth purée by hand or in a food processor.

2   Cream the purée with the margarine until light and fluffy, then add the banana. Stir in the flour, soya flour, carob, baking powder and salt. Add the fruit juice to make a soft mixture. Mix in the chopped nuts.

3   Line a 17.5 cm (7 in) shallow dish with greaseproof paper. Spoon in the mixture, then ≈ FULL for 7 mins. 600W *(6 mins. 700W; 8½ mins. 500W)*, giving the dish a quarter turn once every 2 mins.

4   Leave to stand for 5-10 mins, then turn out onto a wire rack to cool. Peel off the greaseproof paper at the end of the standing time to prevent it sticking.

★ **Preparation:**
15 minutes, plus cooling

≈ **Cooking time:**
10 minutes

⊘ **Power setting:**
FULL

◎ **Serves 8-10**

★ Drain the cooked dates if necessary, as the purée should be thick and not runny like a sauce.

Illustrated opposite

Clockwise from the top: **Date and carob slice** *(see above)*; **Flapjacks** *(see p. 112)*; **Currant biscuits** *(see p. 112)*

Currant biscuits

INGREDIENTS

50g (2 oz) sunflower margarine
50g (2 oz) pear and apple spread
100g (4 oz) wholewheat flour
5ml (1 tsp) orange juice
5ml (1 tsp) orange rind
25g (1 oz) currants

Soft biscuit doughs work well in the microwave, especially if they are a dark colour to begin with, and relatively high in fat and sugar. Although they are less crisp than conventional biscuits, they take only a fraction of the time to cook.

1 Cream the margarine and the pear and apple spread together until smooth. Beat in the flour, orange juice and rind. Work in the currants.

2 Roll out the dough thinly and cut out 12 small biscuits about 5cm (2 in) in diameter.

3 Arrange in a circle on a sheet of greaseproof paper. Cover with absorbent paper and a plate. ≋ FULL for 2½ mins. 600W (*2 mins. 700W; 3 mins. 500W*).

4 Leave to stand for 5 mins. then cool on a wire rack.

★ **Preparation:** 15 minutes

≋ **Cooking time:** 2½ minutes

⊘ **Power setting:** FULL

◎ **Makes 12**

≋ Take care not to overcook. The biscuits should be soft at the end of the cooking time, and will harden as they cool.

Illustrated on p. 111

Flapjacks

INGREDIENTS

75g (3 oz) margarine
40g (1½ oz) brown sugar
175g (6 oz) oats
15ml (1 tbsp) honey

Flapjacks contain a high proportion of fat and sugar and so work successfully in the microwave. They do tend to soften and become more crumbly during storage so don't leave too long an interval before eating them.

1 Put the margarine in a medium dish and ≋ FULL for 1 min. 600W (*30 secs. 700W; 1 min. 500W*). Mix in the remaining ingredients, stirring thoroughly.

2 Press the mixture into a 22.5 x 17.5cm (9 x 7 in) shallow dish and level the surface. ≋ FULL for 3 mins. 600W (*2½ mins. 700W; 3½ mins. 500W*).

3 Press down the top with a fork and leave to cool in the dish. While still slightly warm, mark into fingers with a knife.

★ **Preparation:** 5 minutes

≋ **Cooking time:** 4 minutes

⊘ **Power setting:** FULL

◎ **Makes 9**

★ Substitute molasses for the honey to darken the colour of the flapjacks.

Illustrated on p. 111

MAKING THE MOST OF YOUR MICROWAVE OVEN

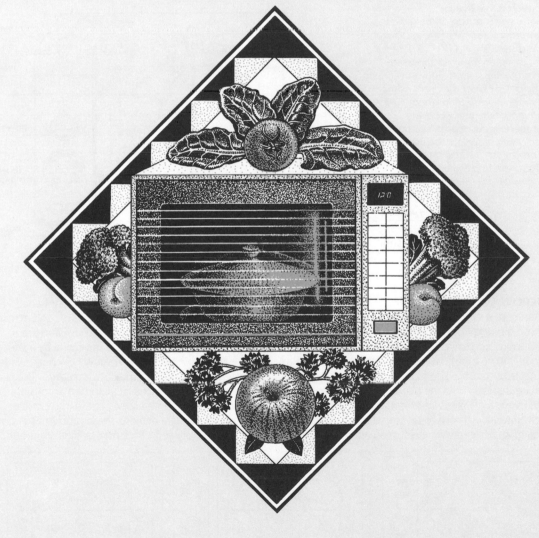

To appreciate all the capabilities of your microwave oven, it helps if you have some knowledge of how microwaves cook food, understand why certain techniques and utensils are employed, and know what the features on a microwave oven are for. All these aspects are explained clearly in the following pages without blinding you with science. There is also practical advice to help you adapt recipes, make full use of produce from your freezer and generally exploit your microwave oven to its full potential.

Understanding microwave ovens

The microwave oven is a revolutionary electrical appliance that can cook, defrost and reheat foods with incredible speed and efficiency. But despite its increased popularity, it is probably the least understood of all kitchen appliances. Its mechanics and facilities are explained in more detail on the following pages but, basically, instead of generating heat like a conventional oven, it generates microwaves. These agitate the molecules in foods at such an incredibly high speed they create instantaneous heat and start the cooking process, as shown opposite.

Microwaves themselves are high-frequency electro-magnetic waves of energy present in the atmosphere, similar to those that convey radio, television and radar signals. They are invisible and non-accumulative, unlike x-rays, gamma rays and ultra-violet rays, which can build up and cause irreversible damage to cellular and chemical structures in our bodies. But because microwave ovens are so different from conventional ovens, they are often regarded with unnecessary wariness. In fact, cooking by microwave is far safer than traditional methods that involve direct heat.

The basic microwave oven
All microwave ovens consist of the same basic unit. This may incorporate some of the additional facilities described on pp. 117-118. When the machine is turned on, the microwaves are produced by the magnetron. They travel along the wave guide and enter the oven, as shown here. The stirrer fan distributes them evenly throughout the metal cooking cavity. The specially designed safety door prevents any microwave leakage while the oven is in operation. The air vent allows steam to escape during cooking.

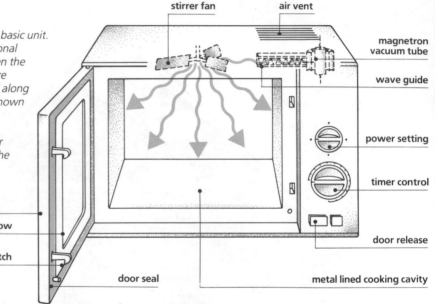

stirrer fan   air vent

magnetron vacuum tube

wave guide

power setting

timer control

oven door

viewing window

door safety latch

door release

door seal

metal lined cooking cavity

HOW MICROWAVE OVENS WORK
The mechanics of a microwave oven are really very simple. The machine is plugged in to the regular domestic electricity supply but converts the electrical energy emitted to electromagnetic waves by passing it through a magnetron vacuum tube. The high frequency microwaves produced are directed into the oven cavity by a wave guide. The oven cavity is made of metal, a material which reflects microwaves without absorbing them. So once the door is closed and the machine is turned on, all the

microwave energy produced is safely contained within the cooker. The microwaves bounce off and across the oven's metal walls in a regular pattern and are distributed evenly throughout the cavity by a stirrer fan.

The three diagrams below show how microwaves react to different materials in the cooking cavity. They can be reflected, transmitted or absorbed according to the composition of the items they come into contact with. Microwave cookery exploits these properties in order to cook food safely and efficiently, as explained opposite.

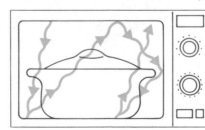

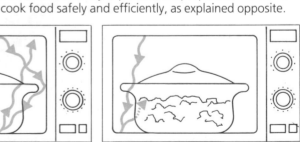

Reflection
Microwaves are reflected by metal; they cannot pass through it. Microwaves bounce off the metal surfaces (walls, ceiling and floor) of the oven cavity in a regular pattern.

Transmission
Microwaves are transmitted by other materials, such as glass, ceramics, paper and some plastics. Microwaves can pass through these substances without heating them up.

Absorption
Microwaves are absorbed by the moisture molecules contained in foods. The microwaves can only penetrate to a depth of about 5cm (2 in) but the rest of the food heats through by conduction.

HOW MICROWAVES COOK FOOD

The unique properties of microwaves allow them to cook foods directly without heating up the cooking cavity. Microwaves are absorbed by the moisture molecules — water, fat and sugar — contained in foods. They make the molecules vibrate at an intense rate, millions of times per second, which causes friction and generates heat as shown below. The heat spreads rapidly through the food from the microwaves' initial point of penetration, which is all over the surface to a depth of about 5cm (2 in), with one layer heating up the next by conduction. Those microwaves that do not hit the food initially continue being reflected to and from the oven's metal walls until they do penetrate the food.

Microwave energy is absorbed at different rates depending upon a food's density and composition. Foods which contain a lot of air, moisture, sugar or fat cook faster by microwave energy than foods that have a dense molecular structure, which takes longer to penetrate and heat through, (see pp. 124-125).

Microwaves pass through certain materials, such as glass, china, paper, and some plastics, without being reflected or absorbed by them. Items made from these materials make suitable utensils for microwave cookery as they do not use up any of the microwave energy produced, allowing it all to pass through to the food. Consequently, containers made from these materials remain comparatively cool, although they may heat up through conduction by being in contact with hot food.

Items made from or containing metals should never be used in microwave ovens. The fact that metals reflect microwaves means that they do not allow the energy to reach food but reflect it away. This can cause sparking in the oven cavity, disturb the carefully balanced electro-magnetic field and the magnetron, and thus seriously damage the oven.

How microwaves affect food molecules

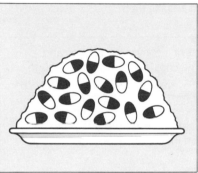  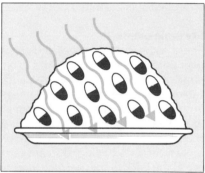

1 All foods are composed of thousands of molecules; in particular, water, fat and sugar molecules which all attract microwave energy.

2 A pulse of microwave energy is absorbed by a piece of food and has the effect of aligning all the molecules in one direction.

3 The next pulse of microwave energy reverses their direction. This happens millions of times per second, producing instant frictional heat.

ARE MICROWAVE OVENS SAFE?

A microwave oven is one of the safest kitchen appliances you can have. Unlike a conventional cooker, it has no hot surfaces either inside or outside the machine; there are no naked flames and items are safely contained within the cooking cavity. The microwave oven casing is designed to be sturdy and stable so you cannot accidently tip one over.

Tests, standards and maintenance

All microwave ovens undergo stringent tests at the manufacturers for both electrical safety and microwave leakage (the most common anxiety). These include opening and closing the door 100,000 times to simulate many years of usage. Tests are carried out after every 10,000 such operations to check that there is no deterioration in the machine's safety level.

Those models designed for domestic use that comply with national electrical safety standards will also have been independently tested and approved by the relevant government agency. All such microwave ovens have many special safety features. They have a series of door locks and switches that make it impossible to operate the oven unless the door is properly shut. Special tests are carried out on each of these locking devices. In particular, to check that if one interlock fails, the magnetron will immediately stop producing microwaves. Microwave oven doors are constructed to precise specifications to ensure that once they are shut, the cooking cavity is completely sealed against energy leakage, and when opened, the machine's generation of microwaves immediately ceases.

Provided you comply with the manufacturer's recommendations for installation, usage and maintenance (see p. 119), your microwave should remain safe to use for many years. If your microwave oven becomes damaged in any way, do not use it until it has been repaired and checked by one of the manufacturer's qualified service technicians. Never attempt to repair it yourself.

Choosing a microwave oven

When it comes to buying a microwave oven, there appears to be a bewildering range to choose from. They can be portable or built-in; they have different capacities, wattages and systems of power control; they may offer a choice of additional features as shown opposite; or even combine microwave power with conventional cooking facilities. Your choice will depend upon such factors as size, price, availability and how you plan to use the microwave power. Consider your present and your future needs: how many people will be using the oven; what other cooking facilities you have, etc. After examining different models for their facilities, do check that your choice complies with national safety standards and has good servicing arrangements.

TYPES OF MICROWAVE OVEN

There are four basic categories of microwave oven as described and illustrated below.

Portable ovens

These come in various sizes and wattages. The larger the oven, the higher the output has to be. Installation is straightforward. They simply require a firm work surface, table or trolley to stand on and a nearby electrical socket. Some models can be built into your kitchen units so long as you ensure that there is sufficient space between the machine's air vent and any neighbouring surfaces so that air can circulate freely and steam can escape. If the vents are at the back of the machine, don't push or fit it against a wall; if they're on top, don't put the machine directly under a shelf or cupboard.

Two-level microwave ovens

Some microwave ovens are fitted with a shelf which allows cooking on two levels. In this type of oven, the microwave energy usually enters the oven cavity through the sides rather than the top. About 60 percent of the energy is fed to the upper section of the oven and 40 percent to the bottom part. Foods which require more microwave energy for thorough cooking can be placed on the shelf, while those needing slower, gentler cooking can be put on the floor of the oven. This type of microwave gives greater flexibility, especially if you want to cook a whole meal at one time or if you regularly cook for a number of people, but it does need a certain amount of planning and calculation. Also, with more food in the oven, cooking times will be longer than in other types of microwave oven. Shelves cannot be added to other models, they can only be used in microwave ovens that have been designed to take them.

Double-oven units

Double units consist of a conventional oven and a microwave oven. The cooking operations are quite separate, but the two are situated conveniently close together. Food can be microwaved for speed, then browned in the conventional oven or under the grill. You can, however, use a portable model with an existing conventional oven in much the same way.

Combination ovens

Combination ovens provide microwave and conventional cooking facilities in the same oven cavity. They are particularly good for roasting and baking, as you can combine fast cooking in the microwave with conventional browning. A whole meal can be produced in a very short time, but with all the look of traditionally baked food. The microwave and conventional cooking facilities may be simultaneous or in sequence, depending upon the model. You can also use them separately. The microwave ovens maximum output, however, is usually lower than in portable or double-oven models.

Types of microwave oven
Microwave ovens can be grouped into the four categories shown here.

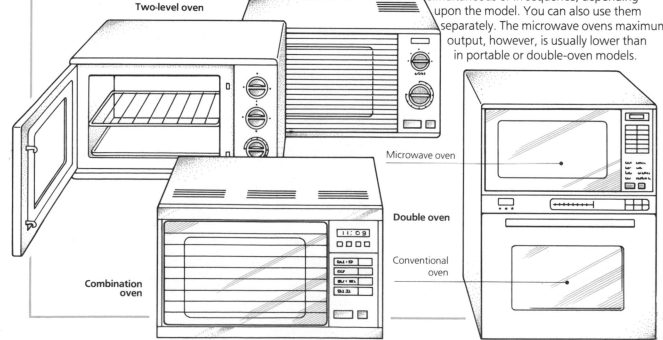

Two-level oven

Portable oven

Microwave oven

Double oven

Conventional oven

Combination oven

ADDITIONAL FEATURES ASSESSED AND EXPLAINED

Most microwave ovens, whatever category they come under, also incorporate some or all of the following features. Consider these carefully when making your choice and select those that will suit your needs: for example, if you frequently use frozen foods, a separate Defrost button is an advantage. You should also consider the design of the controls and make sure you understand how to operate them. Some of the more technologically advanced systems may seem rather daunting.

Features to look for
Check the diagram and the notes below to help you decide which features will be useful to you. Gauge the oven's capacity by the size of container it will accommodate. A power output between 500W and 650W is adequate for all foods, particularly if you have three or four power settings.

Temperature probe
Only useful if you want to monitor foods by temperature.

Turntable
Useful provided it can be removed. Other models may incorporate a rotating antenna to distribute energy more evenly (see p.118).

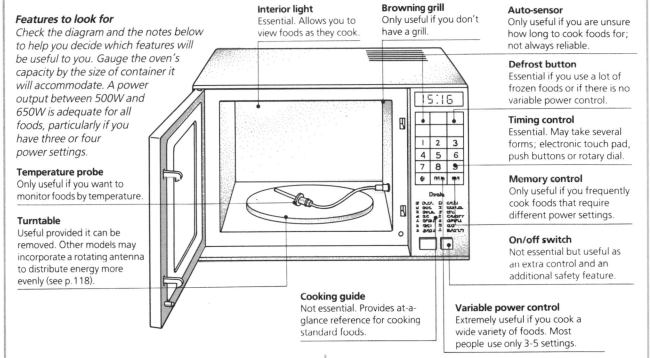

Interior light
Essential. Allows you to view foods as they cook.

Browning grill
Only useful if you don't have a grill.

Auto-sensor
Only useful if you are unsure how long to cook foods for; not always reliable.

Defrost button
Essential if you use a lot of frozen foods or if there is no variable power control.

Timing control
Essential. May take several forms; electronic touch pad, push buttons or rotary dial.

Memory control
Only useful if you frequently cook foods that require different power settings.

On/off switch
Not essential but useful as an extra control and an additional safety feature.

Cooking guide
Not essential. Provides at-a-glance reference for cooking standard foods.

Variable power control
Extremely useful if you cook a wide variety of foods. Most people use only 3-5 settings.

Timing control

In microwave cookery, control is by time rather than by temperature and most microwave ovens incorporate some means of time control. This may be set by a touch pad, push buttons or a dial. Some controls can be set very accurately to as little as one second, others are programmed in minutes. Once the cooking time is set, the timer works back to 0 and a bell, buzzer or pinger will alert you when the cooking time is completed. The timer will also turn off the microwave energy automatically at the end of the cooking period. If you find you frequently require timings in seconds and your oven cannot set them, invest in a mechanical cooking timer that registers seconds.

Interior light

This lights up the cooking chamber once the machine is turned on and enables you to keep an eye on foods as they cook. It goes off automatically when the cooking time is completed and the oven has turned itself off.

Defrost button

Most microwave ovens have a separate Defrost facility. This lowers the microwave energy emitted either by pulsing it on and off in a regular pattern, or by reducing the overall wattage. Less energy is necessary to ensure that frozen foods are completely thawed rather than just thawed on the surface, and to prevent them from starting to cook at the edges before the centre has thawed. On models that do not offer variable power control, the Defrost setting can also be used to cook and reheat foods at a more gentle speed.

On/Off switch

Some models require a power On button to be operated separately once the cooking and timing controls have been selected, the food placed in the cavity and the oven door closed. This often turns on the interior light and a cooling fan, which prevents the electrical components becoming overheated and helps to disperse steam. The Off switch turns the power off during cooking if desired. It is really supplementary to the Door Release button, which cuts off all circuits before the door can be opened, but it acts as an additional safety control.

Memory control

A few models have a memory control panel which can store instructions for cooking at a particular power level for a specified amount of time. Other models incorporate memory controls that allow you to select a series of cooking times at different power levels; the oven will start with one then move on to the next. These models also offer delayed start so you can leave foods to cook while you are out or busy with other tasks. Check that such controls are not overly complicated.

Auto-sensor

An auto-sensor microwave is controlled in a slightly different way from other microwave cookers. You indicate on the control panel the type of food that is going to be cooked. The machine calculates the required cooking time by measuring air temperature and the amount of steam released during cooking, and switches off automatically when the food is done.

Cooking guide

The oven fascia may have a display guide showing the different power settings available and the types of cooking they are most often used for.

Temperature probe

Some ovens incorporate a temperature probe which has a flexible connection to a socket inside the cooking cavity. The probe is usually used for cooking meat, but can be used with other foods. The point of the probe is inserted into the food and is left in position throughout the cooking process. The degree of cooking is selected and when the required temperature is reached, the microwave either turns off automatically or reduces the power setting to keep the food warm.

Browning grill

Some models have a browning grill element fitted into the roof of the oven cavity. Although this is less powerful than a conventional grill, it can be used for browning foods before or after cooking. When using this facility, however, you should take care to use a suitable container.

Turntable

Many ovens incorporate a revolving turntable on the floor of the oven. This may be instead of or as well as a stirrer fan to aid the even distribution of microwaves through the cooking cavity. Turntables are usually made of toughened ceramic glass and can be removed for cleaning, or if you want to use a large or awkwardly-shaped container. You should never put a dish on the turntable if it is going to knock against the oven's walls as it rotates during cooking. Check in the manufacturer's instruction guide that the turntable is removable and that the oven operates effectively without it.

Rotating antenna

This is a slatted metal disc which may be concealed below the oven floor or above the ceiling. It rotates, driven by air from the cooling system, and helps to distribute the microwaves more evenly around the cooking cavity.

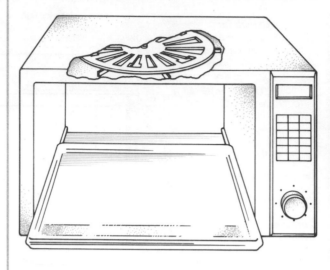

Rotating antenna and removable floor
Microwave ovens that don't have a turntable may incorporate a rotating antenna and a removable floor instead. The antenna is another device designed to aid the distribution of microwaves.

Removable floor

Some microwave ovens without a turntable have a ceramic glass tray on the floor of the oven. Usually this is sited just above the oven's base to allow microwaves to be reflected. This type of floor acts as a spillage tray and can be removed and washed when necessary.

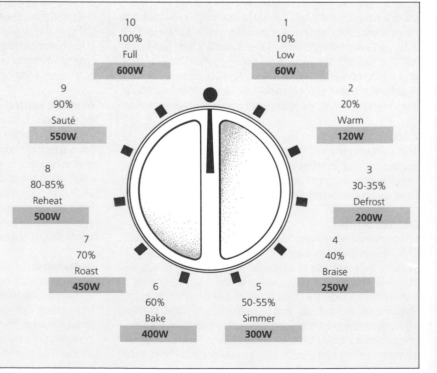

VARIABLE POWER CONTROL
Many microwave ovens offer a choice of anything up to ten different power settings. These provide you with far greater control of cooking and allow you to cook foods at a slower rate when this is necessary. However, power levels in different models have not been standardized and settings may be indicated in numerals, percentages, wattages or by various cooking descriptions. On most models, you can reduce or increase the cooking power by adjusting the control at any time during the cooking programme.

Comparative power settings
The dial shows the different systems commonly used by manufacturers. The most accurate guide is by wattage.

Setting	Percent	Description	Wattage
10	100%	Full	600W
1	10%	Low	60W
9	90%	Sauté	550W
2	20%	Warm	120W
8	80-85%	Reheat	500W
3	30-35%	Defrost	200W
7	70%	Roast	450W
4	40%	Braise	250W
6	60%	Bake	400W
5	50-55%	Simmer	300W

Cleaning and maintaining your microwave oven

As you unpack your new microwave oven, inspect it for damage and check that all the components you expect are there. Pay particular attention to the oven door, seal and hinges, and to the oven interior, which should not be dented or scratched in any way. Do not attempt to repair any damage yourself. Always contact the manufacturer or dealer if you have any worries or problems. Follow the manufacturer's recommendations for installation, then carefully read the instructions.

IMPORTANT POINTS TO REMEMBER

● Never turn the oven on when it is empty. Always put a mug of water in the oven cavity when it is empty if there is any chance that it may be switched on inadvertantly.

● Never use the oven cavity as a storage cupboard.

● Never use a microwave oven to dry or heat clothes, papers or any items other than food.

● Never put any undue strain upon the door; for example, by hanging towels from it.

● Never attempt to close the oven door when there is an object between it and the oven or the door seal may be damaged.

● If the door seals or latches look damaged, do not use the oven until a service engineer has checked and replaced them.

● Do not tamper with the machine in any way, either with its casing or controls.

● Only use qualified technicians when the machine needs repairing or servicing.

Cleaning a microwave oven

Clean the exterior occasionally by wiping with a damp cloth. Take care not to splash water onto or into the vents. The interior walls do not heat up so any splashing or spilling of foods that occurs during cooking does not get baked on to the surface and can be quickly wiped off. It is important to keep the oven cavity clean as any foods that do get spilled will absorb microwave energy and slow down the cooking process.

Follow these cleaning guidelines:

■ First, turn off the electrical supply to the machine.

■ Use a damp cloth to wipe over all the interior surfaces and the door after each use. Do not use cleansing agents unless the manufacturer recommends any.

■ Take out and clean any removable parts such as turntable, ceramic tray, shelves, at regular intervals.

■ If a stain proves difficult to remove, heat a bowl of water in the oven to boiling point. The steam produced should loosen the food particles. Wipe off with a damp cloth. Use a cloth soaked in warm soapy water to wipe off greasy stains. Then wipe with a rinsed cloth.

■ Pay particular attention to the oven door seal area. This should be kept spotlessly clean by wiping with a cloth soaked in warm, soapy water, then with a rinsed cloth and finally with a dry cloth.

■ To remove lingering smells from the oven, place a bowl containing three parts water to one part lemon juice in the oven cavity and heat on ⊠ FULL for about 5 minutes. Wipe and dry the oven surfaces afterwards.

■ Never use a knife, scouring pad or any abrasive cleaners in the microwave as these will scratch surfaces and thus damage the oven by distorting the wave patterns of the microwaves.

How to clean your microwave oven

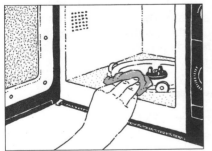 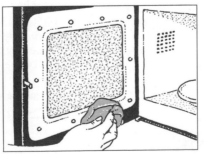 

The cooking cavity
Clean the cooking cavity frequently with a cloth soaked in warm soapy water. Take out and clean any removable parts.

The door seals
Keep the door seals spotlessly clean. Use a mild detergent, rinse and wipe dry. Never use abrasive materials.

Removing stains
Stubborn stains should be loosened by bringing a bowl of water to the boil in the oven. Then clean in the normal way.

Microwave tools and equipment

O ne of the great advantages of a microwave oven is the wide range of utensils and containers you can use. In many cases, foods can even be cooked in the same dishes you wish to serve them in. Although a growing range of specialist microwave equipment is available in the shops, on most occasions you should be able to manage with equipment already in your kitchen cupboards.

CHOOSING EQUIPMENT FOR THE MICROWAVE

When deciding which container to use, your first consideration should always be whether it will allow the microwaves to pass through it onto the food. Suitable equipment is made from glass and ceramic, natural substances such as paper, straw and cotton, and certain plastics. It should not contain any materials that will reflect or absorb microwaves. Metal dishes should never be used as metal reflects microwaves and so prevents the food from heating up. More importantly, the introduction of metal into a microwave oven will cause sparking (arcing) which can damage the oven walls and cause pitting. Pitting will alter the pattern of the microwaves and so affect the oven's performance. In some cases, severe sparking may even damage the magnetron. Select items from those shown here and overleaf.

Pottery and china

Containers made of sturdy china or pottery are suitable for microwave cookery. Ordinary china cups and plates can be used as long as they do not have any metal trimmings, such as a gold or silver pattern. When using china crockery, check that there isn't any gold lettering on the underside or metal screws in the handles. Do not use fine porcelain as this could be damaged in the microwave. Fully glazed earthenware and stoneware can be used, but food in these dishes may take slightly longer to cook as these materials are often slightly absorbent. Avoid using unglazed earthenware as this is porous and will absorb microwaves, becoming extremely hot and slowing up the cooking process.

china cup

china plate

china mug

Glassware

Glass dishes are ideal for microwave cookery. They transmit microwaves and allow you to keep an eye on foods as they cook. When cooking foods with a high fat or sugar content, use heatproof glass as these foods can reach such high temperatures in the microwave oven. Heatproof glass measuring jugs, soufflé dishes, basins and flan cases are all particularly suitable. Never put lead crystal in the microwave for obvious reasons.

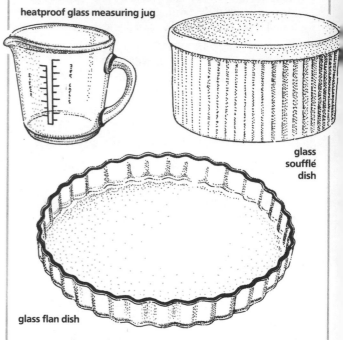

heatproof glass measuring jug

glass soufflé dish

glass flan dish

Paper and cardboard

Absorbent kitchen paper and plain white paper napkins are very useful for soaking up excess moisture while microwaving foods, particularly when defrosting breads and cakes, or baking potatoes. They can also be used to prevent foods like pastry cases drying out too much during cooking. Don't use patterned or coloured absorbent papers as the dyes can transfer to foods or the oven base during the heating process. Greaseproof paper is good for lining loaf and cake dishes, and also for covering foods. Cardboard containers can be used in the microwave, although those with waxed linings should only be used for defrosting as the heat emitted by foods as they cook may melt the wax.

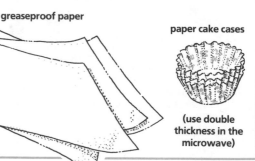

greaseproof paper

paper cake cases

(use double thickness in the microwave)

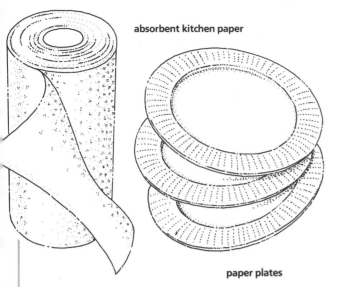

absorbent kitchen paper

paper plates

Wood, straw and linen

Equipment made from wood or straw can be used in the microwave oven for reheating foods such as bread rolls, but should not be used for long periods of cooking or they will dry out and eventually split. Wooden spoons may be left in the microwave for short periods of time when making sauces, although the handles start to get hot after about 2 minutes. Pure linen cloths and napkins may be used to line bread baskets or to wrap foods for short periods. Check that they do not contain synthetic fibres.

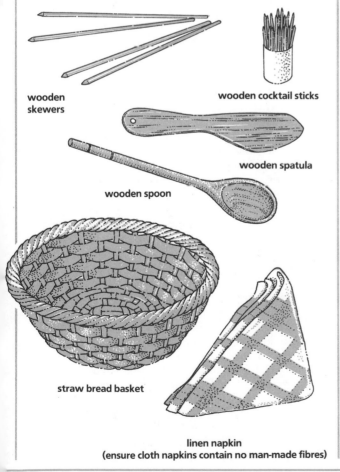

wooden skewers

wooden cocktail sticks

wooden spatula

wooden spoon

straw bread basket

linen napkin
(ensure cloth napkins contain no man-made fibres)

Plastics

Rigid plastic containers and utensils that are labelled dishwasher-safe are usually designed to withstand high temperatures and can be used in the microwave too. Articles made from polypropylene and polysulfone are made in a range of shapes and sizes and these are suitable for freezer-to-microwave cookery. There is also a wide choice of specialized microwave cookware made from plastic, as shown overleaf. Lightweight plastic containers, such as yogurt or margarine tubs, can be used for defrosting but are unsuitable for cooking foods as they are likely to distort and may melt when the food becomes hot. Plastic microwave boiling bags and roaster bags make good containers, though they always should be pierced or fastened loosely so steam can escape during cooking. Be sure to secure the bags with plastic tags not metal ones, or use string or rubber bands. Ordinary plastic bags are not suitable for cooking

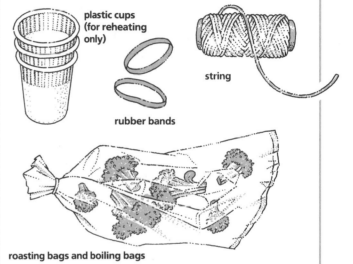

plastic cups
(for reheating only)

string

rubber bands

roasting bags and boiling bags

The use of **plastic cling film** in the microwave is a contentious subject at the moment. There has been increasing concern about this product and it is currently undergoing stringent tests and investigation. It has been noted that some of the plasticizer di-2-ethyhexyladipate (DEHA) used to soften plasticized polyvinyl chloride film (commonly known as cling film) can migrate into closely wrapped foods, and the level of migration is markedly higher as foods increase in temperature. As a result of these findings, many authorities now recommend that cling film should not be used in the microwave oven. If you do use it, avoid letting it come into direct contact with foods as they cook. Manufacturers are now producing a polythene film which does not contain these additives and it is thought that this can be used safely in microwave cookery. Alternatively, make use of boiling bags, paper, casserole lids and plates when you want to cover foods.

polythene cooking wrap

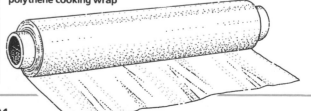

Special microwave cooking equipment
A wide range of containers made from thermoplastics and glass-ceramics are designed specifically for microwave cookery.

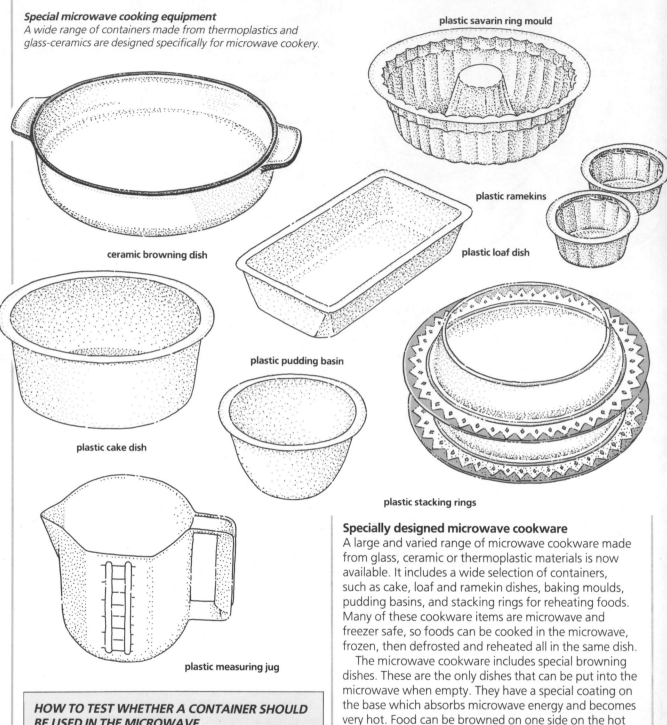

plastic savarin ring mould

plastic ramekins

ceramic browning dish

plastic loaf dish

plastic pudding basin

plastic cake dish

plastic stacking rings

plastic measuring jug

HOW TO TEST WHETHER A CONTAINER SHOULD BE USED IN THE MICROWAVE
If you are not sure about using a dish in the microwave oven, you can carry out a simple test to check its suitability and efficiency. Place the dish in the microwave, then put a glass jug containing about 300ml (½ pint) water in the dish and ≅ FULL for 1-2 minutes. At the end of the cooking time, if the dish is cool and the water in the jug is hot, the dish is suitable. If the dish is hot and the water is still cool, the dish should not be used as it contains moisture which is attracting some of the microwave energy and preventing it reaching the food.

Specially designed microwave cookware
A large and varied range of microwave cookware made from glass, ceramic or thermoplastic materials is now available. It includes a wide selection of containers, such as cake, loaf and ramekin dishes, baking moulds, pudding basins, and stacking rings for reheating foods. Many of these cookware items are microwave and freezer safe, so foods can be cooked in the microwave, frozen, then defrosted and reheated all in the same dish.

The microwave cookware includes special browning dishes. These are the only dishes that can be put into the microwave when empty. They have a special coating on the base which absorbs microwave energy and becomes very hot. Food can be browned on one side on the hot surface, then turned over and browned on the other. The side done first is usually the brownest. Microwave cooking can then continue in the same dish. Once food is added to the dish, the microwaves are attracted to the food rather than the coating. Do not cover food in a hot browning dish with absorbent paper as it may scorch.

Microwave roasting racks made from a ceramic or rigid plastic material are also available. Although these are designed for cooking meats by raising them out of their cooking juices, they are effective for baking cakes and breads and vegetable loaves, in fact anything that benefits from all round microwave energy.

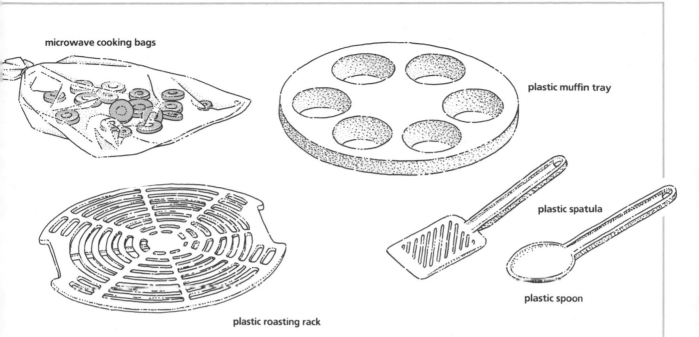

microwave cooking bags

plastic muffin tray

plastic spatula

plastic spoon

plastic roasting rack

CONTAINER SHAPES

The speed that foods cook at will be affected by the type of container and its shape. China and pottery, for instance, are slower cookers than special microwave plastic dishes. Round dishes give better results than rectangular ones in which food tends to overcook in the corners, where it receives more microwave energy. Ring moulds are extremely effective in microwave cookery as they provide even heat distribution and allow microwave energy to reach foods on all sides and in the centre. You can easily improvise this shape by standing a plain glass tumbler in the centre of a round dish. Hold the glass in position while you surround it with food.

Choose deep bowls or dishes when cooking foods that require a large quantity of fast boiling water, for example pasta, pulses or rice, otherwise the water may boil over. Allow space for foods to swell or rise during cooking. Pasta, pulses and grains all expand as they cook, and milk-based sauces swell as they heat up. When cooking these items, they should only take up half to two-thirds the volume of a container. For other foods, make sure that the dish is not too large or the food will spread out thinly and overcook at the edges before the centre has been cooked. A medium-sized shallow dish is suitable for most of the recipes in this book. Avoid using narrow-necked containers when heating liquids as the steam produced may not be able to escape fast enough and the container may explode due to the build up of pressure. Do not use tall, narrow dishes for heating food either as it will be packed into too dense a mass to cook evenly.

WHAT NOT TO USE IN THE MICROWAVE

Never use the following in a microwave oven:

● Metal dishes, such as baking trays, loaf tins and foil trays, or dishes with metal trims. Anything metal will reflect the microwaves and cause sparking. Use special microproof bakeware instead.

● Unglazed pottery and earthenware. These attract the microwave energy, becoming very hot, and will slow down the cooking of food.

● Melamine containers. These attract microwave energy and may melt or become charred.

● Dishes that have been repaired with glue or that have glued handles as the glue may absorb microwave energy and melt.

● Tall, narrow-necked containers which may cause steam to build up dangerously.

● Wire fasteners on paper or plastic bags. The metal in the fastener becomes hot and could spark off a fire.

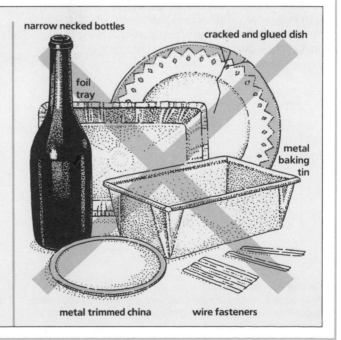

narrow necked bottles

cracked and glued dish

foil tray

metal baking tin

metal trimmed china

wire fasteners

Factors that affect microwave cooking

M any factors affect the length of cooking time required by different foods in the microwave oven: the machine itself; the nature of the food and the quantity; the container used and the recipe method. All these factors have to be taken into consideration for a recipe to work successfully in your microwave oven.

The microwave oven itself

Microwave ovens have yet to have their power levels standardized, so one machine can vary from another in power output, even if both have the same wattage and are made by the same manufacturer. Machines offering variable power control also use different systems to describe their various power levels (see p.118). Whenever you consult microwave recipes, check how the power levels recommended in them compare with those of your own oven and make any necessary adjustments. The recipes in this book use four different power levels as shown on the chart on p.28. Compare these levels to the wattages offered on your microwave oven and select the nearest appropriate setting. In the recipes and cooking instructions provided, the alternative times given in brackets for 700W and 500W machines are the lowest times recommended to avoid any possibility of overcooking. You can always extend the cooking time but you can't rescue overcooked foods.

Although most microwave ovens now have stirrer fans, turntables or rotating antennae to help distribute the microwave energy evenly, models may still have individual hot spots—areas in the oven where food will cook faster. To check if your oven has hot spots, put equal amounts of water in nine cups, mugs or other small containers, all made of the same material. Space them out over the base of the oven as shown below, then turn on to full power. Watch carefully to see which container comes to the boil first and note that this is the hottest spot in the oven. Techniques like turning the dish, stirring or rearranging the food during cooking (see pp.126-128) are designed to ensure that food cooks evenly, despite the existence of any hot spots in the oven.

Testing for hot spots
By heating up nine identical cups with equal amounts of water, as described above, you can find out your oven's hot spots and then arrange foods accordingly.

Starting temperature of food

The higher the starting temperature of food, the faster it will heat up and cook in the microwave. Foods taken out of the refrigerator and put straight into the microwave will take longer to cook than foods that are allowed to come to room temperature first. You may even find that the same foods take slightly longer to cook on cold days than on hot ones. It is important always to follow the instructions for temperatures of ingredients in recipes, for example, when the addition of boiling stock is recommended, do use boiling stock. Adding cold stock will slow down the cooking process and affect all the recommended cooking times in the recipe.

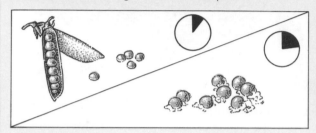

Food temperature
The colder a food is, the longer it will take to cook. Frozen peas need a minute or so more than fresh.

Composition of food

Different components in the food also affect the cooking time. Foods with a high fat and sugar content will reach higher temperatures and cook at a faster rate than other foods because fats and sugars absorb microwave energy more quickly. Consequently, items with a sweetened fruit filling will cook more quickly than similar-sized ones with a low-fat savoury filling. Note that particular care is needed when reheating and serving foods with jam-type fillings as the jam will heat up much faster and become scalding hot while the outside remains quite cool.

Foods that have a high liquid content, such as soups, take longer to cook than foods that cook by their own moisture content. Always add the minimum amount of water when cooking vegetables, whether fresh or frozen, as the more water you add, the slower the cooking time will be, and the more nutrients you will lose in the cooking water.

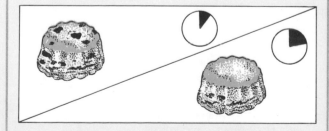

Food composition
A sweetened scone heats up slightly faster than a plain scone because of its higher sugar content.

Density of food

Density is the most important factor in determining the cooking time of food in the microwave. Dense foods take longer to cook than foods identical in size that have a loose, airy structure; for example, fibrous root vegetables take longer to cook than bread rolls. The dense nature of the food slows down heat conduction. When you are cooking a mixture of dense and light-structured foods, try to arrange the denser foods around the edge of the dish where they will receive more microwave energy. Place light-structured foods in the centre so that they don't cook too quickly.

When you are microwaving a dense quantity of food, such as a vegetable and nut roast, the centre is always the slowest part to cook through because the microwave energy only penetrates the surface to a depth of 5cm (2 in). If possible, use a round, shallow dish or a ring mould for such foods. Alternatively, place the dish on an upturned plate or a microwave roasting rack so that more microwave energy can reach the centre from underneath.

The density of the container used will also affect the cooking time: foods take longer to cook in heavy china than in a glass dish or special microwave plastic container.

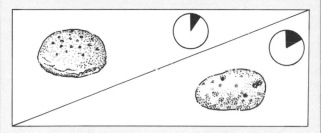

Food density
A light and airy bread roll needs less time to heat up than a potato, which is denser.

Size and shape of food

Always cut food into uniform shapes and sizes for even cooking in the microwave. Small or thin pieces cook faster than large, thick pieces. If cooking irregular shapes, such as broccoli, place the thinner or less solid area toward the centre of the dish and the thick stalks on the outer edge of the dish. The same principle applies to delicate areas, such as asparagus tips, which would overcook and spoil if exposed to too much microwave energy. With these foods, you may wish to shield the delicate areas from the microwaves for part of the cooking time (see p.128).

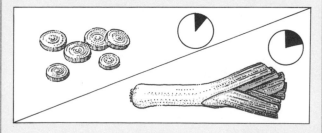

Food size
Vegetables sliced to a similar size cook faster and more evenly than whole vegetables.

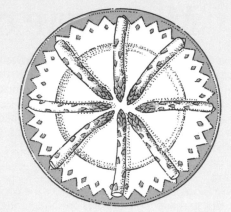

Food shape
Thick areas of food take longer to cook than thin areas. Put thicker parts around the edge of the dish.

Quantity of food

In microwave cookery, the cooking time is dependent on the amount of food in the oven, unlike a conventional oven which will take the same length of time to cook eight potatoes as it does to cook one. This is because the same amount of microwave energy has to be absorbed by fewer or more items.

Most of the recipes in this book are for four people, but you can reduce the amounts successfully for one or two people by following certain guidelines. When reducing the quantity, use a smaller dish so that the food does not spread out any more than in the original recipe.

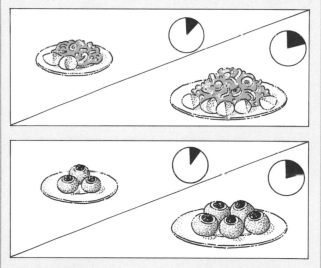

Food quantity
The larger the amount, the longer it will take to cook by microwave power.

Remember that when the amount of food is reduced the microwaving time will have to be reduced too, though not in direct proportion. If halving a recipe, cook for approximately two-thirds of the original time; if quartering it, cook for approximately one-third of the original time. Test the food a minute or two before the estimated time to avoid overcooking it. Cover, stir and rearrange the food as directed in the original recipe.

Microwave cooking techniques

Most of the techniques employed in microwave cookery are similar to those used in conventional cookery. They are designed to promote even cooking, to speed up cooking processes, to accelerate or lessen evaporation and to improve the finish of the cooked item. For the best results, use them whenever a recipe recommends and they'll soon become second nature.

Covering

Covering foods in the microwave reduces the cooking time, helps to retain moisture and prevents spattering of the oven walls. As a general guide, food that is usually covered for conventional cooking is likely to be covered in the microwave too. Items such as vegetables and stewed fruit are best cooked covered, but items that are meant to have a dry finish, such as biscuits or bread, are better left uncovered. Casserole dishes with lids made of suitable (non-metallic) materials are ideal for microwave cookery. If your dish doesn't have a lid, put a plate or a saucer over it. Alternatively, use a microwave bag or polythene cooking wrap as a cover.

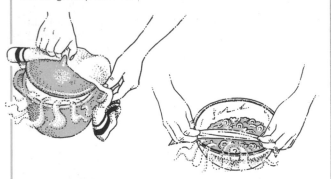

Uncovering foods
Lift covers away from you to avoid scalding steam.

Always take great care when removing a lid or cover at the end of the cooking time as you will release a cloud of scalding steam. Lift it away from you, using oven gloves, to avoid receiving any steam burns to your face or arms.

Instead of cooking vegetables in a covered dish, you can place them in a boiling or roasting bag. Remember to pierce the bag in a few places first, or tie it loosely at the neck so that steam can escape. This is a particularly good method for cooking whole vegetables such as cauliflower.

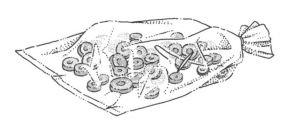

Boiling bags
These are excellent for cooking vegetables.

Greaseproof paper can also be used for covering foods during cooking, but make sure that it doesn't become loose and flap around, particularly if the oven has a strong fan. Secure it with wooden cocktail sticks if necessary.

Pastry flan cases cook more successfully when covered with absorbent paper and a plate. This produces comparatively dry results without the pastry becoming unpleasantly hard.

Piercing

A considerable build-up of steam can occur during microwaving, so any food items with a tight-fitting skin or membrane, such as whole fruit, vegetables or raw egg yolk, must be pierced before being cooked in the microwave to prevent them exploding. Fruit and vegetables can be pierced with a fork or the tip of a sharp knife; egg yolks are best pierced with a cocktail stick. As stated above, boiling bags and cooking wrap must either be pierced or secured loosely so some steam can escape.

Piercing
Always pierce foods that have skins and membranes.

Wrapping

The microwave process brings out the moisture content of foods, drawing it to the surface. As a result, items that you want to cook with a dry surface, such as baked potatoes, benefit from being wrapped in absorbent paper while they cook. This soaks up most of the excess moisture produced and helps to spread the heat more evenly over the food. Always remove the paper once you've taken the food out of the oven or it may stick.

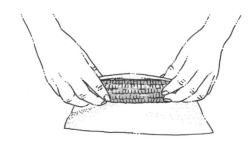

Wrapping
Wrap foods in absorbent paper to soak up moisture.

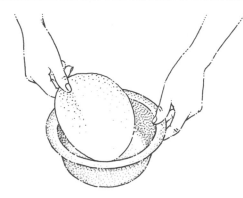

Lining
Line cake dishes with greaseproof paper.

Lining dishes

Cake dishes should be lined with greaseproof paper as specified in the recipe. Remove the lining paper after the standing time has been completed to prevent it sticking to the cake. Do not grease cake dishes or coat them with flour as this results in an unpleasant film on the cake.

Stirring

Stirring is one of the most important techniques in microwave cookery. As microwaves only penetrate food to a depth of about 5cm (2 in), the food at the edges of the dish may cook before food in the centre, especially if the food is dense in structure. To prevent food at the edges overcooking before the centre is ready, dishes should be stirred at frequent intervals or as directed in recipes. Stirring should be from the outside edges inwards, so that the heat is distributed equally to the centre. Stirring sauces in this way also prevents lumps forming, although continuous stirring is not necessary in microwave cookery.

If you are cooking something that requires stirring several times during cooking, one method is to divide the total amount of cooking time and set the timer at regular intervals so that you will be reminded to stir at the end of each block of time.

Even if your microwave has a turntable, it is still a good idea to stir foods when advised to do so.

Stirring
Stir from the edges to the centre for even cooking as directed in recipes. Stirring is equally important when reheating and defrosting foods.

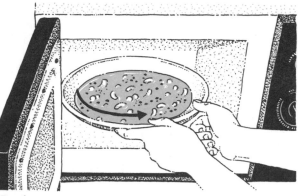

Turning
Turn cakes, pies, and whole dishes at regular intervals.

Turning or rotating

To ensure even cooking, foods that cannot be stirred, such as lasagne, moussaka, vegetable loaves and cakes, need to be given a half or quarter turn at intervals throughout the cooking time as specified in the recipes. This is usually unnecessary if your oven has a turntable.

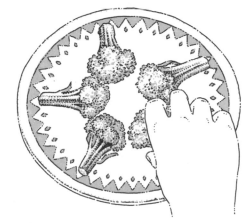

Arranging
Arrange foods in circles, not rows. Place denser areas at the edge and more delicate areas in the centre.

Arranging

In microwave cookery, food has to be arranged carefully to ensure even cooking. Always place denser, thicker items at the edge of the dish so they receive more microwave energy. When cooking several items of the same food, arrange them in a circle around the edge of a plate or in a round dish. Space them out evenly so that the microwave energy reaches all sides. Leave the centre of the dish empty as this area receives less microwave energy while the edges receive equal amounts. Make sure that the food is an even depth in the dish, and spread it out in a shallow dish rather than piling it up in a deep container. Denser items such as vegetable loaves often benefit from being cooked in a ring mould so that microwaves can penetrate directly from the centre as well as from the edges.

When reheating an individual meal on a plate, arrange the food so that it is evenly spread out with denser foods on the outside and more delicate items in the centre.

Turning over

Large solid items, such as baked potatoes, aubergines or whole cauliflowers, should be turned over halfway through the cooking time unless otherwise specified in the recipe. This allows all sides and surfaces to receive even exposure to the microwaves.

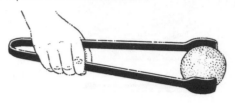

Turning over
Turn over large, whole items for even cooking.

Rearranging

To ensure that no food stays in a hot spot in the oven for the whole of the cooking time, you need to rearrange foods that cannot be stirred. Baked potatoes and aubergines can be moved around in the dish or on the base of the oven at the same time as turning them over. Move items from the edge to the centre, from the back to the front, etc, so that nothing remains in the same position throughout the cooking time.

Rearranging
Move foods from the edges to the centre.

Shielding

Delicate or thin areas of food that are in danger of overcooking before the rest of the food is ready, can be shielded from the microwaves for part of the cooking time with small, smooth strips of aluminium foil. This is the only time that foil should be used in the microwave, but you should check your manufacturer's instructions before using it. The amount of food left uncovered must be much greater than the area shielded by foil.

You can add the foil at the beginning of the cooking time and remove it halfway through, or it can be added to areas once they are cooked.

Shielding can be useful when you are using a square or rectangular container, to prevent the corners from overcooking. Arrange the foil as illustrated.

The foil strips must always be secured firmly. Wooden cocktail sticks are good devices to use. Do not use plastic ones as they could melt from being in contact with the hot food. The foil must never be allowed to touch the sides of the oven cavity or it could cause sparking. If any piece of foil becomes loose, switch off the microwave power immediately and remove it.

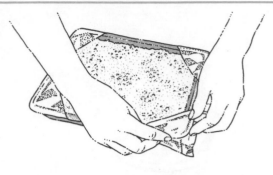

Shielding
Use strips of foil to prevent corners burning.

Standing time

Standing time is an essential part of microwave cookery as food continues to cook by conduction of heat after it has been removed from the microwave or the microwave power has been turned off. Some foods, such as cakes, may still look uncooked when they come out of the microwave but will firm up and dry out as they finish cooking through during the standing time. Removing food while it is still slightly undercooked or underthawed and allowing it to finish by standing prevents the edges becoming overcooked by being exposed to further microwave energy before the centre has cooked through.

Standing times vary considerably and depend upon the density and volume of different foods. Vegetables need very little standing time; cakes usually need between 5 and 10 minutes. As a rule, the denser the food, the longer the standing time required.

Recipes will state when standing times are necessary so follow their recommendations and don't judge a food until after it has completed its standing time. When further cooking is required in the microwave, there is usually no need to repeat the standing time.

Tenting

If food requires a long standing time to complete the cooking process, it should be covered with a tent of foil to maintain its temperature. Smaller items of food such as baked potatoes, stuffed peppers and corn-on-the-cob, can be wrapped in foil, shiny side inwards so it reflects the heat, and they will stay hot for at least 20 minutes while other dishes are prepared. The foil must be removed if they are returned to the microwave oven.

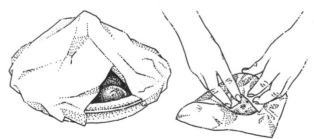

Tenting
Enveloping foods in foil helps to retain their heat once they have been removed from the oven.

Browning

Because foods cook so quickly by microwave energy, the surfaces are not exposed to heat changes in the normal way so they do not dry out and brown as they would in a conventional oven. Consequently, foods such as cakes and breads may look paler and unappetizing compared to traditionally baked products, even though their flavour is just as good.

Fortunately, you can improve the appearance of such foods in a variety of ways:

▨ Use wholewheat flour in cakes, pastry and bread. These are all items that remain very pale when cooked in the microwave. Using wholewheat flour immediately gives them a better colour as well as more flavour and nutritional value.

▨ Add dried fruit, such as apricots or dates, or chopped nuts and seeds, to breads and cakes for extra colour.

▨ Decorate pale cakes with slices of fresh fruit or a colourful topping using natural fruit juice and not artificial food colouring.

▨ Sprinkle loaves and scones with poppy seeds, toasted sesame seeds, cracked wheat or oatmeal before baking.

▨ Sprinkle cakes or biscuits with chopped nuts, toasted desiccated coconut, ground cinnamon or poppy seeds.

▨ Add carob powder, cocoa, or ground cinnamon to cake and biscuit mixtures with the flour to make them darker.

▨ Put gratin-style dishes with a grated cheese topping under a preheated conventional grill to brown. Deduct this grilling time from the standing time.

▨ Microwave browning dishes, which have a special coating that enables the base of the dish to become very hot, can be used for browning microwave "toasted" sandwiches, nut rissoles and cutlets, onions, etc.

Testing

When testing food to see if it is cooked, it is important to remember that it continues to cook for some time after it has been taken out of the microwave oven. If it is not cooked enough for your liking after completion of the recommended standing time, return it to the microwave oven for another minute or two. Use the following guidelines when deciding if items are cooked:

▨ Microwave vegetables until they are just tender when pierced with a fork. If you cook them until they are soft, they will have overcooked by the time they are served.

▨ Cakes, particularly sponges, look unpleasantly wet on top at the end of the recommended cooking time. By the end of the standing time they should look dry and be thoroughly cooked. Test them at the end of the time by inserting a wooden cocktail stick or fine skewer into the centre. If it comes out clean, the cake is cooked. If it is slightly coated, put the cake back in the microwave for a few minutes more, stand for 5 minutes then test again.

▨ Pastry flan cases are cooked when the pastry looks opaque. If cooking in a glass dish, you can double check by seeing if the base looks dry from underneath.

▨ Quiche fillings may look soft and wet on top after the recommended cooking time, but they dry out after a few minutes standing time.

REHEATING FOOD

Cooked food reheats extremely well by a low level of microwave energy. Flavour, colour and texture remain as if freshly cooked, and the fast reheating time ensures that fewer vitamins are lost than when food is reheated in a conventional oven. The techniques used for cooking foods in the microwave also apply when reheating them.

Vegetable casseroles or vegetables in a sauce reheat better than vegetables on their own. Do not put them into too large a dish or the sauce will spread and dry out at the edges. Any foods in a sauce should be loosely covered during reheating. Dry foods with a crisper finish can be reheated covered in absorbent paper.

Soups are easy to reheat in individual portions, either in a mug or a bowl, and take only a few minutes depending on the thickness of the soup. Stir the soup when it starts bubbling up at the edge of the container, then cook for another minute or so to allow it to heat through to the centre.

Always take care when reheating anything with a jam or other high-sugar filling as this will become very hot very quickly while the outside may still feel cool.

When reheating plates of food, make sure that the food is evenly distributed on the plate, with the thicker items on the outside edges. Up to three plates of food can be heated at a time in an average sized oven. Position them one on top of the other using special microwave stacking rings. Alternatively, cover the first plate with another upturned plate or large soup bowl and place the next plate on top of this. Avoid positioning the plates so that the same items of food are directly above one another. Give the plates a half turn every few minutes in the same way as you would for cooking. The food is reheated when the bottom of the plate feels warm.

Stacking rings
These separate plates of food during reheating.

Converting recipes for the microwave

There is no need to abandon all your favourite conventional recipes when you want to use your microwave oven. Recipes for foods that are naturally moist or cooked by boiling, steaming or poaching can all be adapted quite easily and successfully for the microwave, usually just by reducing the cooking time and the liquid content. However, it's best not to attempt to adapt recipes until you feel fully familiar with your microwave and understand the different microwave techniques, knowing just when and why they should be employed. The only way to do this is by practice and experimentation.

For the best results when converting a conventional recipe, use an existing microwave recipe with similar ingredients and quantities as a model, refer to pp. 9-27 for ingredients' cooking times and techniques, and keep to the following guidelines.

■ Preparation is usually the same for microwaved food as for conventionally-cooked food, only it is far more important that ingredients such as vegetables are cut to a small and uniform size for the microwave.

■ Foods that are normally cooked covered should be covered in the microwave.

■ When cooking a variety of ingredients in a dish, remember to stir it through every few minutes in the microwave.

■ Dishes that cannot be stirred, such as flans, should be turned every few minutes to promote even cooking.

■ When cooking separate food items, remember to follow the rules for arrangement (see pp. 127-128) and to rearrange them during the cooking time.

■ As a general guide, reduce the amount of liquid required in a conventional recipe by a quarter or a third. More liquid can always be added during the cooking period if necessary.

■ For steamed vegetables, put them in a bowl with 30-45ml (2-3 tbsp) water and they will steam themselves.

■ Cut the cooking time by at least a half, although there is no standard rule on this. Follow the timings used in a comparable existing microwave recipe rather than guessing them.

■ Always underestimate the cooking time and test frequently for readiness. Take particular care when cooking foods like eggs, milk and custards, and foods with a high fat or sugar content, as they cook so quickly.

■ Remember that foods will continue to cook after being removed from the microwave and allow for this. The denser the food, the longer the standing time required.

■ Casseroles and bakes cook very quickly in the microwave but often improve in flavour by being cooked some time in advance and then being reheated so that flavours have time to develop and blend together.

■ You may prefer to add more herbs and spices to some dishes than you would when cooking them conventionally as the quick cooking times do not allow their flavours to permeate through a dish in the same way. Test for taste and adjust seasonings to suit your palate.

■ Do not add salt at the beginning of the cooking time as it has a dehydrating effect. Add to taste before serving.

■ Cake and pudding mixtures should be slightly wetter than in conventional recipes. Because they rise so much in the microwave, only half fill containers with the raw mixture. Allow them to finish cooking through by standing for 5 to 10 minutes.

■ Pastry cases must be baked blind before being filled. Cover with absorbent paper and a plate to keep fairly crisp. Allow for shrinkage.

■ Pulses should be presoaked in the normal way.

■ Cook pulses, grains and pasta in the microwave in the usual amount of boiling water. Use slightly larger containers than usual to allow for swelling and prevent the fast-boiling water spilling over.

■ Red kidney beans should be boiled rapidly for the first 10 minutes. I recommend you do this conventionally on the hob.

WHICH FOODS WILL WORK IN THE MICROWAVE

A wide range of foods cook extremely well in the microwave, but you must accept that this is a different method of cooking requiring a new approach and yielding cooked foods that may look and taste slightly different to those you are used to .

■ Whole fruits and vegetables cook very successfully in the microwave. The flavours tend to be fresher and the texture slightly different; for example, baked potatoes do not become crisp. Remember when baking whole fruit and vegetables that the skin must be pierced beforehand or steam will build up and cause them to burst during cooking.

■ Ready-prepared sweet and savoury dishes cook well by microwave energy, but the finish may look pale. These can often be browned under a conventional grill if you prefer.

■ Nut roasts and grain savouries cook well, provided the raw mixture is well flavoured and quite moist.

■ Casseroles and pulse dishes benefit from being made in advance and then reheated so that their flavours have time to develop.

■ Most cake and bread mixtures bake successfully by microwave, though the raw mixture should be slightly wetter than in conventional recipes. Allow for considerable rising, and see p. 129 for tips on improving their appearance.

■ Pastry cases work well when cooked blind and covered with absorbent paper and a plate. Do not make their fillings too moist, and never fill a raw pastry case or the pastry will become soggy.

■ Steamed puddings cook very quickly in the microwave and have a good texture.

■ Pasta, grains and pulses will cook in the microwave, but be sure to cook them in ready boiling water (see p.130), and do not attempt to do too much at one time. If you want to cook more than 225g (8 oz), it's better to boil them conventionally.

■ Arrowroot, agar agar and stockcubes can all be dissolved in minutes.

■ Milk can be infused in minutes.

FOODS THAT CANNOT BE COOKED IN THE MICROWAVE OVEN

Some recipes and cooking techniques will not work in a microwave oven and should not be attempted.

● Eggs cannot be hard-boiled. The pressure of steam inside the egg shell would cause it to explode.

● Batters and pancakes cannot be microwaved successfully as they will not become crisp and dry.

● Deep-frying should not be attempted as it is impossible to control the temperature of the oil.

● Double-crust pies rarely work successfully as the fillings tend to cook much faster than the pastry.

Cooking for one

M icrowave cookery is a marvellous way to cook for one. It makes it easy to prepare quick, healthy snacks and meals so you can avoid resorting to convenience foods, biscuits and cakes when you want to eat in a hurry. Vegetable dishes can be made in minutes from whatever ingredients you have on hand. Cook them in a little stock or sauce to make a simple casserole, or steam them and enjoy their full, fresh flavours. To make a more substantial meal, bake a potato while you are preparing the vegetables, or if you have any leftover cooked grains, pasta or pulses in the refrigerator, they can be reheated in minutes and will taste as if freshly cooked. Garnish the dish by adding a few chopped fresh herbs, toasted nuts or grated cheese for extra nourishment and flavour.

Most dishes can be cooked in the dish or container you want to serve them in, which means that you save on messy washing up. The microwave also allows you to cook small portions without any worry of them burning as they often do on the hob. Nor do you have the cost of heating up a conventional oven just to cook one portion of food. You can cook small quantities of any of the recipes in this book. Remember to reduce the cooking time accordingly: for half the quantity, cook for approximately two-thirds of the original time; for a quarter of the quantity, cook for approximately one-third of the original time.

If you have a freezer too, cooking for one with a microwave becomes even more economical. You can take advantage of seasonal gluts and bargains, blanch vegetables in the microwave (see p. 134) and then store them in the freezer until you are ready to use them. You can bake several portions or dishes at a time when you are in a cooking mood, and then freeze for future use. Read the notes on freezing and defrosting on the following pages.

Menu-planning

W hen you want to combine several dishes into a meal, you'll need to plan the order in which you cook them because the timing factor is so important and varies from food to food. Take your time and read through the recipes carefully, taking note if some dishes are marked as being better cooked in advance or served after being reheated.

Many food items can be reheated as required. One of the major benefits of the microwave is that most dishes that are reheated remain moist and taste freshly cooked. However, vegetables are less flexible because they cook so quickly and although reheating is possible, they can easily become overcooked.

The fact that denser foods require standing times means that you can microwave any accompanying vegetables after the main dish has been removed from the oven. On the other hand, the more dense vegetables like baked potatoes, corn-on-the-cob and vegetables that have been stuffed, will retain their heat for about 20 minutes once cooked if you wrap them in foil after removing them from the microwave.

Recipes containing egg or cheese do not usually reheat well; they cook so quickly it is very easy to overcook them, so dishes that include these as ingredients are usually better cooked just before serving. Dishes that have cheese as a garnish can always be cooked in advance without the cheese, and then the cheese can be added for reheating.

Grains, pulses and pasta all reheat well by microwave. You may even prefer to cook them conventionally and just use the microwave to reheat them before serving.

Cook foods in the dishes you plan to serve them in whenever possible as this helps to retain their heat. Single portions can be served onto a plate for the latecomer and then simply covered and reheated when required.

The microwave and the freezer

The microwave and the freezer are perfect partners. Both help to keep flavour, texture and vitamin loss in foods to a minimum and both are great time-savers as well as being economical. The great advantage of using a microwave oven in combination with a freezer is that it can defrost food in a matter of minutes; eliminating the need to pre-plan and take foods out of the freezer hours before they are required in order for them to defrost. Some foods, particularly vegetables, can even be defrosted and reheated in one action. You can also blanch small quantities of vegetables in the microwave in minutes for storage in the freezer as described on p. 134.

The recipes in this book that freeze well are marked with a blue symbol. Make sure that all dishes are thoroughly chilled before freezing. Use rigid containers for soups and sauces and allow room for expansion. Seal all items tightly and label. Test for flavour during reheating and add more seasoning if necessary.

Defrosting and reheating foods

Most microwave ovens have a Defrost control which allows food to defrost slowly and evenly without danger of it drying out or cooking at the edges. If your microwave oven doesn't have a special Defrost or comparably low setting, you can simulate the Defrost control by turning the oven on to Full power for 30 seconds and then off for 1½ minutes. Repeat this process until the food is almost defrosted and allow it to thaw completely by standing. Even with a Defrost control, you'll find that certain, denser foods need additional resting times to prevent the edges cooking while the centre still has to thaw.

Follow the defrosting guidelines below and you should have perfect results every time.

▨ Defrost food in a container the same size as the block of food. If the food has too much room it will spread out as it melts and the edges will start to cook.

▨ Loosen lids of containers, but leave the food covered.

▨ Break up blocks of food as they start to defrost, so that the frozen parts are brought to the edges.

▨ Stir stirrable foods from the edge to the centre as they start to thaw.

▨ Foods that cannot be stirred should be separated out, turned over and rearranged to ensure even defrosting.

▨ Pies and cakes should be given a quarter turn every minute or so during defrosting.

▨ When defrosting food in a bag, pierce or slit the bag to prevent it bursting.

▨ Flex bags during defrosting to rearrange the food inside and speed up the process.

▨ Shield any delicate areas with small pieces of foil to prevent them cooking while denser parts are still thawing.

▨ When defrosting frozen foods that you do not want to cook or reheat, such as soft fruit, use only the Defrost setting. If the food starts to feel warm, leave it to stand for a few minutes then continue defrosting in the microwave.

▨ Place breads, cakes, biscuits or pastry on a double layer of absorbent paper, so that any excess moisture is absorbed and the food does not become soggy.

▨ Vegetables can be cooked directly from the freezer without being defrosted first (see pp. 10-19).

▨ As the defrosting process continues after foods have been removed from the oven, do not wait until foods are completely defrosted before removing them or the outer edges may start to cook.

▨ Always remove food from foil containers and remove any metal ties from plastic bags before putting in the microwave to defrost.

Defrosting and reheating chart

FOOD	QUANTITY	MICROWAVING TIME	METHOD
Soup	300ml (½ pint)	⚌ FULL for 4-6 mins. 600W *(3-4 mins. 700W; 5-7½ mins. 500W)*.	Place in a serving dish, allowing room for bubbling. Break up and stir 2-3 times.
	600ml (1 pint)	⚌ FULL for 7-10 mins. 600W *(5-8 mins. 700W; 8-12 mins. 500W)*.	
Sauces	300ml (½ pint)	⚌ FULL for 5-6 mins. 600W *(4-5 mins. 700W; 6-7½ mins. 500W)*.	Place in a dish that fits, allowing room for bubbling. Break up and stir 2-3 times.
	600ml (1 pint)	⚌ FULL for 10-12 mins. 600W *(8-10 mins. 700W; 12-15 mins. 500W)*.	
Butter	225g (8 oz)	⚌ DEFROST for 1½ mins. 600W *(1-1½ mins. 700W; 2-2½ mins. 500W)*. Leave to stand for 5 mins.	Remove any foil wrappers. Give a half turn and turn over halfway through.
Yogurt	150ml (¼ pint)	⚌ FULL for 1 min. 600W *(30 secs. 700W; 1 min. 500W)*.	Remove lid or turn out of container and place in bowl. Stir and serve.

FOOD	QUANTITY	MICROWAVING TIME	METHOD
Vegetable casseroles	4 portions	⊠ FULL for 15-16 mins. 600W (*12-13 mins. 700W; 18-19 mins. 500W*).	Place in a shallow dish and cover. Give the dish a half turn every minute until defrosted enough to stir gently to break up then stir once or twice.
Moussaka, lasagne	4-portion size	⊠ DEFROST for 8 mins. 600W (*6½ mins. 700W; 12 mins. 500W*). Leave to stand for 6 mins. then ⊠ DEFROST for 5 mins. 600W (*4 mins. 700W; 7 mins. 500W*), then ⊠ FULL for 9 mins. 600W (*7½ mins. 700W; 11 mins. 500W*).	Place in a shallow dish and cover. Give the dish a half turn every 2 mins.
Vegetable loaves and bakes	450g (1 lb) 4-portion size	⊠ FULL for 5-8 mins. 600W (*4-7 mins. 700W; 6-10 mins. 500W*).	Place in a dish that fits, and cover. Give the dish a half turn every 2 mins.
Plated meal	1 portion	⊠ DEFROST for 4 mins. 600W (*3-4 mins. 700W; 6 mins. 500W*). Leave to stand for 4 mins, then ⊠ DEFROST for 4 mins. 600W (*3-4 mins. 700W; 6 mins. 500W*).	Cover with an upturned plate. Test by feeling the base of the plate; when it feels hot the food should be ready.
Rice, cooked	100g (4 oz)	⊠ DEFROST for 2 mins. 600W (*1½ mins. 700W; 3 mins. 500W*). Leave to stand for 2 mins. then ⊠ FULL for 1½ mins. 600W (*1-1½ mins. 700W; 1-2 mins. 500W*).	Place in a shallow dish and cover. Break up with a fork halfway through the time and before the start of the standing time. Stir at the end of the reheating time.
Pasta, cooked	300g (10 oz)	⊠ DEFROST for 10-12 mins. 600W (*7-10 mins. 700W; 15-18 mins. 500W*).	Place in a shallow dish and cover. Stir 2-3 times
Biscuits	225g (8 oz)	⊠ DEFROST for 1 min. 600W (*30-60 secs. 700W; 1½ mins. 500W*). Leave to stand for 5 mins.	Turn over halfway through. Remove any foi wrappings
Bread, large unsliced loaf	1	⊠ DEFROST for 7-9 mins. 600W (*5-7 mins. 700W; 10-14 mins. 500W*). Leave to stand for 5-10 mins.	Turn over and rearrange twice.
Large sliced loaf	1	⊠ DEFROST 11-12 mins. 600W (*9-10 mins. 700W; 15-18 mins. 500W*). Leave to stand 10-15 mins.	Turn over and give loaf a half turn several times.
Bread rolls	2	⊠ DEFROST for 30-60 secs. Leave to stand for 2-3 mins.	Place on absorbent paper.
	4	⊠ DEFROST for 1½-3 mins. Leave to stand for 2-3 mins.	Place on absorbent paper. Rearrange halfway through.
Fruit cake	1	⊠ DEFROST for 5 mins. 600W (*4 mins. 700W; 7 mins. 500W*). Leave to stand for 10 mins.	Give a half turn halfway through defrosting time.
Scones	2	⊠ DEFROST for 1-2 mins. Leave to stand 1-2 mins.	Place on absorbent paper. Turn over and rearrange once.
Fruit (soft fruit, eg raspberries, etc.)	225g (8 oz)	⊠ DEFROST for 3-5 mins. 600W (*2-4 mins. 700W; 4-7 mins. 500W*).	Stir gently once or twice. Leave to stand until completely thawed.
	450g (1 lb)	⊠ DEFROST for 6-8 mins. 600W (*5-7 mins. 700W; 7-10 mins. 500W*).	As above
Fruit juice concentrate	1 can 200ml (7 fl oz)	⊠ DEFROST for 2-3 mins. 600W *2 mins. 700W; 3-4 mins. 500W*.	Remove from can if made of metal. Allow to stand for 3-5 mins.
Fruit purée	600ml (1 pint)	⊠ DEFROST for 10 mins. 600W (*8 mins. 700W; 12 mins. 500W*).	Stir several times. Allow to stand for about 10 mins.

Blanching fruit and vegetables for the freezer

A microwave oven takes much of the effort out of blanching vegetables and is a boon to people who grow their own produce. Vegetables can be picked at the peak of perfection and then blanched in small quantities in the microwave. When blanching large amounts, it is usually better to use conventional methods.

Blanching is necessary to stop enzyme activity in vegetables and fruits which would otherwise continue even at freezer temperature, causing loss of flavour and texture. Deterioration is noticeable in some produce after only a few days. Others will last longer but the eating quality will not be so good.

Before blanching, clean, trim and slice the vegetables to a uniform size. To blanch 450g (1 lb) vegetables, place in a casserole dish or bowl with 45ml (3 tbsp) water. Cover and cook on FULL for the time specified on the chart. Stir halfway through the blanching time.

Drain then plunge into iced water to prevent further cooking. Once chilled, drain well and pack into freezer bags, or boiling bags if you want to reheat them in the microwave. For smaller amounts, put the prepared vegetables into a boiling bag. Do not add any water. Secure the bag loosely with a non-metallic fastener and cook on FULL for the appropriate time, turning the bag over halfway through. After the blanching time, put the bag into iced water. Keep the top of the bag above the surface and leave open to allow steam to escape. Once the vegetables have chilled, secure the bag tightly, wipe dry and freeze in the normal way.

Most blanched produce will keep for up to a year in the freezer. Do not thaw before cooking or more vitamin content will be lost and the texture will be poor.

Blanching chart

VEGETABLE 450g (1 lb)	MICROWAVING TIME on FULL
Broad beans	3 mins. 600W *(2½ mins. 700W; 3½ mins. 500W)*
Green beans, *whole*	3 mins. 600W *(2½ mins. 700W; 3½ mins. 500W)*
sliced	2 mins. 600W *(1½ mins. 700W; 2½ mins. 500W)*
Broccoli florets	2½-4 mins. 600W *(2-3 mins. 700W; 3-5 mins. 500W)*
Peas	2 mins. 600W *(1½ mins. 700W; 3-5 mins. 500W)*
Carrots	3½ mins. 600W *(3 mins. 700W; 4 mins. 500W)*
Corn-on-the-cob *(2)*	7 mins. 600W *(6 mins. 700W; 8½ mins. 500W)*
Courgettes	3 mins. 600W *(2½ mins. 700W; 3½ mins. 500W)*
Cauliflower florets	3 mins. 600W *(2½ mins. 700W; 3½ mins. 500W)*
Brussels sprouts	5 mins. 600W *(4 mins. 700W; 6 mins. 500W)*
Leeks, *sliced*	2-2½ mins. 600W *(1½-2 mins. 700W; 2½-3 mins. 500W)*
Sweetcorn	3 mins. 600W *(2½ mins. 700W; 3½ mins. 500W)*
Asparagus	4 mins. 600W *(3 mins. 700W; 5 mins. 500W)* .
Fennel	3 mins. 600W *(2½ mins. 700W; 3½ mins. 500W)*
Spinach	2 mins. 600W *(1½ mins. 700W; 2½ mins. 500W)*
Beetroot, *small*	5 mins. 600W *(4 mins. 700W; 6 mins. 500W)*
Parsnips	3 mins. 600W *(2½ mins. 700W; 3½ mins. 500W)*
Turnips, *sliced*	3 mins. 600W *(2½ mins. 700W; 3½ mins. 500W)*
Peppers, *sliced*	3 mins. 600W *(2½ mins. 700W; 3½ mins. 500W)*
Onions, *sliced*	2 mins. 600W *(1½ mins. 700W; 2½ mins. 500W)*
FRUIT 450g (1 lb)	**MICROWAVING TIME** on FULL
Apples	3-4 mins. 600W *(2-3 mins. 700W; 3-5 mins. 500W)*
Pears	3-4 mins. 600W *(2-3 mins. 700W; 3-5 mins. 500W)*
Rhubarb	3-4 mins. 600W *(2-3 mins. 700W; 3-5 mins. 500W)*

Blanching vegetables by microwave

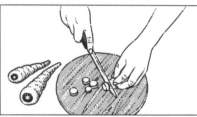

1 Clean, trim and slice vegetables evenly into 5cm (2 in) pieces.

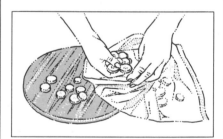

2 Pack into a boiling bag. Secure loosely. Cook on FULL as on chart.

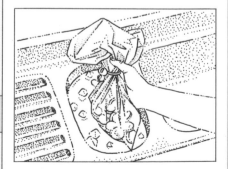

3 Chill thoroughly in iced water. Secure bag tightly, label and freeze.

Hints and tips

BUTTER AND MARGARINE

▩ Use the microwave for softening butter and margarine. For 225g (8 oz) heat on DEFROST for 30-60 seconds. This will speed up the creaming process when preparing cake mixtures.

▩ To melt 100g (4 oz) butter or margarine, place in a dish and ≋ MEDIUM for 1-2 minutes.

BREADS

▩ Heat up rolls and bread before serving with a meal; you can even heat them in their serving basket. Put them in the oven just before you want to serve them as they soon cool down again, and ≋ FULL for 1-2 minutes.

▩ You can freshen bread that has gone slightly stale by heating it on ≋ FULL for about 15 seconds.

▩ Make dry breadcrumbs for coating foods by heating a slice of bread on ≋ FULL for 2-3 minutes. Then crush with a rolling pin or in a blender and store in an airtight container.

▩ You can defrost a single slice of bread in 10-15 seconds. Place it on absorbent paper.

FRUIT

▩ Soften dried dates to make chopping easier by heating on ≋ DEFROST for 30-40 seconds.

▩ Microwave citrus fruit on ≋ FULL for 15-20 seconds to make peeling the rind easier. Prick the skin first.

Drying citrus peel

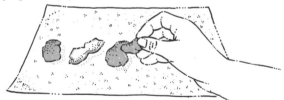

▩ Dry large pieces of peel from citrus fruit to use as a flavouring in teas, cakes and sauces. Orange, tangerine and grapefruit are particularly good. First, make sure that the peel is scrubbed well to remove any traces of chemical pesticides. Lay the pieces out on absorbent paper and ≋ FULL for about 1 minute, until dried and crisp. Rearrange and turn over halfway through the cooking time. Store in an airtight container.

▩ To dry grated peel, place in a bowl and ≋ FULL for 30-60 seconds, or until dry. Stir once.

▩ To extract more juice from citrus fruit, prick the skin in a few places. For each fruit, ≋ FULL for about 30 seconds before squeezing.

▩ Speed up the process of reconstituting dried fruit in the microwave. For 100g (4 oz), place in a bowl with 600ml (1 pint) boiling water. Cover and ≋ FULL for 6-10 minutes. Stir, then leave to stand for 10-30 minutes.

HONEY

▩ To restore smooth, runny texture to honey that has crystallized in the jar, place in the microwave (after removing the lid) and ≋ FULL for 1-2 minutes.

SEEDS

▩ Bring out the full flavour of seeds by toasting them in the microwave. For 50g (2 oz) spread on a dish and ≋ FULL for about 2 mins. Stir frequently during this time to prevent scorching.

NUTS

▩ Toast desiccated coconut by spreading 75g (3 oz) over a 22cm (9 in) plate. ≋ FULL for 1-2 minutes or until golden brown. Stir at least once.

▩ To roast whole nuts, spread 100g (4 oz) over a medium-sized plate. ≋ FULL for 3-4 minutes and stir at least twice.

DESSERTS

▩ Soften ice cream before serving by warming on ≋ DEFROST for between 30 and 60 seconds. This timing should also enable you to loosen jellies and mousses from their moulds.

SAUCES

▩ Save on washing up by making sauces in the jug you wish to serve them in. Select a jug large enough to allow for any bubbling and liquid expansion.

▩ To prevent sauces cooking unevenly and lumps forming, watch for the mixture thickening around the edge of the bowl or jug. As this happens, open the door and stir the sauce briskly.

▩ Bring starch-thickened sauces to the boil and remove from the microwave as soon as they have thickened. Overcooking will destroy the thickening agent and the sauce will start to thin.

TOMATOES

▩ To make skinning tomatoes easier, put them into a bowl, cover with boiling water and ≋ FULL for about 30 seconds. Drain and then skin.

Covering pastry

PASTRY

▩ Bake pastry blind by covering with absorbent paper and a plate. This helps to keep the pastry crisp and dry. Avoid adding very moist fillings or the pastry will absorb the moisture and become soggy.

Drying herbs

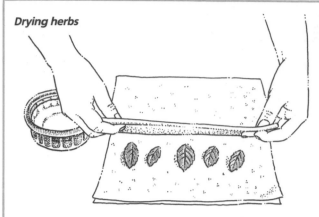

DRYING HERBS

▧ Fresh herbs picked wild or grown in the garden can be dried effectively in the microwave for use all the year round. Dry about 15g (½ oz) at a time. Remove the stalks from the leafy herbs. Rinse the leaves carefully, taking care not to bruise them, then pat dry with absorbent paper. Place the herbs between two sheets of absorbent paper on the floor of the oven. Add a small bowl of water as a safety measure: the moisture content in this small amount of herbs is very low and having the bowl of water in the oven cavity too avoids any danger of the absorbent paper scorching. ▧ FULL for 4-6 minutes, depending on the type of herbs, until they lose their bright colour and become brittle to touch. Rearrange the herbs several times and watch them carefully throughout the cooking time. Leave them to cool, then run through a sieve. Store in an airtight jar in a cool, dark place.

EGGS AND CHEESE

▧ Always pay special attention when cooking eggs in the microwave as timings will vary according to the size, composition and freshness of the eggs. It is better to take them out of the oven slightly undercooked, then they can finish cooking by conduction.

▧ To soften curd or cream cheese for easier spreading or mixing, ▧ DEFROST for 30-60 seconds.

JARS

▧ To scrape the last of the contents from preserves and jams in jars, remove lids and ▧ DEFROST for 30 seconds.

▧ To heat baby foods in the jar. Remove the lid and ▧ MEDIUM for 40-60 seconds. Always test the temperature before serving.

JAM-MAKING

▧ Sterilize jars by half filling with water and heating in the microwave until they reach boiling point. Swirl the water around the whole of the inside of the jar then drain and dry before filling.

▧ To test if a jam has reached setting point, place a small amount on to a cold saucer and leave until cool. Push the surface of the jam and if it wrinkles, it's ready.

WINE

▧ To bring red wine to room temperature, pour into a suitable jug, and ▧ FULL for 10 seconds. Do not leave in the bottle.

CAKE-MAKING

▧ Tap the sides of cake dishes during the standing time to help loosen the cake and bring it away from the edges.

▧ The inside diameter of a cake container should not exceed 20 cm (8 in), or the centre will probably not cook through. Use a ring mould for larger cakes.

▧ To melt carob bars, put 50g (2 oz) in a dish and ▧ MEDIUM for 2-3 minutes.

▧ When baking cakes in the microwave, only half fill the container as the mixture will rise considerably in the oven and cause a mess if it overflows.

FROZEN FOODS

▧ Cook frozen vegetables in their own bags. Pierce the bag first and rest it on a plate.

▧ Freeze foods in small or individual portions for speedier defrosting.

▧ When freezing a casserole, it is a good idea to insert an empty paper cup in the centre so food isn't concentrated there and the defrosting process takes less time.

Improvising a ring mould

IMPROVISING CONTAINERS

▧ To make your own ring mould for cooking nut roasts and grain dishes, stand a glass tumbler in the centre of a round dish. Hold in position when adding food.

▧ Unusually-shaped cardboard boxes can be used to make interesting cake containers. Line with greaseproof paper first. Do not use boxes with wax coatings or metal trimmings.

DRIED MUSHROOMS AND SEAWEEDS

▧ The microwave is ideal for reconstituting these ingredients. See p. 25 for detailed instructions on cooking different varieties.

REHEATING PASTA, GRAINS AND PULSES

▧ With the microwave you can reheat pasta, grains and pulses so that they keep their texture and flavour in full. For one to two servings, place in a dish, toss in a little oil, cover and ▧ FULL for 1-2 minutes.

Microwave troubleshooting guide

Some common questions and problems answered and explained

Q I notice that dish size is always specified in microwave recipes. Is the size more important than in conventional recipes?

A Dish size can make all the difference to a microwave recipe. If the dish is too large the food will spread out and may overcook at the edges before the centre is done. On the other hand, if it is too small or narrow, the food may bubble over the top or be squeezed into a dense mass that may not cook through to the centre. Always use the dish size recommended.

Q I thought that dishes stayed cool in the microwave, yet I find that I frequently need to use oven gloves when taking cooked items out of the oven. Does this mean that I am using the wrong kind of dishes?

A Dishes frequently do become hot from the food conducting heat to them. As long as the food in the dishes is cooking in the times specified in the recipes, it simply means that the hot food is heating the dish. If food is taking much longer than the recipes state, then test the dish to make sure it is suitable, following the instructions on p. 122.

Q I have heard that it is a good idea to keep a cup of water in the microwave oven when it is not in use. Why is this?

A This is a good safety precaution in case the oven is accidentally switched on, and it is a particularly good idea when there are children in the house. If the oven is switched on and there is nothing to absorb the microwaves they will bounce off the walls and floor and may damage the oven. A cup of water will absorb the microwaves, preventing them from causing any damage.

Q Is microwaving a healthier way of cooking vegetables?

A It is the perfect way to cook vegetables as it keeps vitamin loss to a minimum. Water-soluble vitamins, such as vitamin C, are easily lost in cooking water, but because so little water is needed for microwave cooking this loss is kept to a minimum. It can be reduced still further by using the cooking water for stock or soup.

The very fast cooking times also mean that vegetables keep their bright colours and natural crunchy textures. Try to prepare vegetables just before you want to cook them, and serve them as soon as possible after cooking; if they are kept warm for a long time more vitamins will be lost.

Foods can also be cooked with less fat and, because vegetables retain more flavour, very little salt is needed—and fats and salt are both things that nutritionists are urging us to cut down on for good health.

Q Is cooking in the microwave cheaper than using a conventional oven?

A Microwave ovens are much more economical than conventional ones. They cook very quickly, there is no need for preheating and part of the cooking process takes place after microwaving during standing time—using no power at all!

Q How do you convert the timings in recipes that do not give alternative timings for other wattages?

A As a general guide, if recipes have been tested on a 600 watt machine on Full power, then reduce the cooking time by 10 seconds per minute if you have a 700 watt machine. If you have a 500 watt machine, increase the times by 15 seconds per minute, checking frequently to make sure the food does not overcook.

Q If you can sear and brown foods in a special browning dish, why can't you fry foods in them?

A It is impossible to control the temperature of oil in a microwave and this could be dangerous, particularly if deep-frying when a large quantity of oil is used. The only frying that should be done in the microwave is "stir-fry style" using a very small amount of oil. This produces beautifully crunchy, tender vegetables.

Q How safe are microwave ovens?

A All microwave ovens are designed with a safety mechanism that ensures the oven cannot operate unless the door is shut and the Start button has been operated. Opening the oven door immediately stops the generation of microwaves which cannot re-start until the door is shut and the Start control operated again.

When buying a microwave oven, check that the model you wish to purchase is approved by a national electrical safety agency. This means that it has been subjected to stringent tests for safety and microwave leakage, including opening and closing the door 100,000 times — which represents many years of normal wear.

Microwave cooking is also safer as the sides of the oven do not become hot like on a conventional oven, though the floor of the cooker may become warm by conduction.

Q If microwaves can pass straight through glass, what stops them coming through the glass door of the oven?

A The glass panel on a microwave door is covered with a very fine metal mesh screen that is specially designed to prevent the microwaves passing through it, but allows you to see into the oven during cooking.

Is there any way of rescuing overcooked foods?

A Because food cooks so quickly in the microwave, it's always better to undercook and then return food to the oven for another minute or so if necessary. Once overcooked, there is no way of restoring texture and flavour to vegetables. They can, however, be liquidized to make soups or sauces. Overcooked fruits can also be liquidized, then sieved if necessary, to make purées or sauces. Overcooked sponge cakes can be used for trifles, and plain biscuits for making biscuit-crumb bases for flans and cheesecakes.

Q **If my microwave has a Defrost button, do I still need to leave foods to stand during defrosting?**

A It depends on the food. For many items the Defrost power level is low enough to ensure gentle defrosting without switching off the machine during the defrosting time, but with a dense quantity of food, such as a cooked moussaka or lasagne, it is better to allow some standing time during defrosting. This enables the centre to defrost without the edges overheating.

Q **Why is salt added before cooking in some recipes, while others recommend adding it afterwards?**

A Vegetables are usually cooked in very tiny amounts of water, and if salt is sprinkled on the vegetables it will cause dehydration of the surface of the food. If food is cooked in a larger quantity of water and the salt can be completely dissolved, then it can be added before cooking in the microwave.

Q **Why is it possible to use aluminium foil to shield food when you cannot use metal dishes for cooking?**

A Foil is used in very small quantities for shielding. The amount of food unshielded must be greater than the amount covered with foil, so that there is plenty of food to absorb all the microwave energy. This is not the case when metal dishes are used as the microwave energy does not even reach the food.

Q **What should you do if you realize you've put a metal trimmed dish in the microwave and it starts sparking?**

A Switch off the microwave immediately and the sparking will stop. As long as you turn off immediately, you are unlikely to do any harm to the oven, but if sparking is allowed to continue the walls of the cooker may become pitted, and this will distort the microwave pattern. In extreme cases, sparking may even damage the magnetron. If in doubt, have your microwave checked by a qualified engineer—never try and repair or dismantle your microwave yourself.

Q **Why do some sauces and hot drinks bubble over the rim of the container once they have been stirred?**

A When you microwave liquids in a confined space, particularly those with a high milk content, the temperature gets much higher below the surface than on the surface. When you stir it, the gases produced by the heating process escape and spill over the edge. To overcome this problem, never allow liquid to fill a container more than three-quarters and stir at least halfway through the cooking time.

Q **Why was my cake hard and dried by the time it had cooled?**

A This is the result of overcooking. The cake should still look moist when removed from the microwave as it will cook through during the standing time. Always aim to undercook rather than overcook in the microwave and remember not to expect items to look cooked until after their standing times. A cake is ready to come out of the oven when the sides come away from the edge of the container and a wooden cocktail stick inserted in the centre comes out clean.

Q **What does it mean when recipes talk about heat equalizing?**

A Microwaves only penetrate food to a depth of about 5cm (2 in), and this area becomes very hot while the centre of the food is still quite cool. During standing time, heat is conducted through to the centre of the food and the two areas become equally hot.

Q **Why do some cakes rise well in the microwave and then sink after being removed?**

A This is due to overbeating when mixing the cake. Too much air is trapped in the mixture causing it to rise well in the oven, but then the cake sinks as air is released during cooling.

Q **Why do I have to extend the cooking time when I am cooking a larger quantity of food than that in a recipe?**

A When microwaves enter the food they have to spread themselves through the total quantity for the food to cook. On the whole, microwave ovens should only be used to cook moderate quantities—up to four to six portions at a time.

Q **Can I heat up plates in the microwave?**

A Yes, so long as they are microwave proof and don't contain any metal. Stack up to six plates, putting a little water between each one and sprinkling some water on the top one. FULL for up to 1 minute. Remember to wear oven gloves when removing them and dry off any excess water.

Glossary

Arcing
Small sparks that occur in the oven cavity during cooking when an electric discharge is conducted from one surface or electrode to another. This may be caused by metal being introduced into the oven either as foil, a utensil or a container. Never use metal utensils in a microwave. Only use foil in small amounts as advised in the manufacturer's instruction manual, and never let it come near to or in contact with the oven walls.

Arcing may also be the result of scratches or indentations on the oven cavity's surfaces; care must be taken when cleaning the oven interior. Always wipe or soak off spilt foods (see p. 119) as carbonization can cause sparking.

Audible reminder
A bell, buzzer or pinger that sounds to let you know when the cooking time set has been completed.

Blanching
Process of boiling vegetables or fruit for a brief period to halt enzyme activity before freezing. See p. 134 for detailed instructions on blanching vegetables in the microwave.

Browning dish
A special dish with a tin-oxide coating on its base designed to brown or crisp foods in the microwave oven. The coating absorbs microwave energy and becomes very hot when preheated in the oven. These dishes come in a variety of shapes and sizes and can be used with a lid for sautéing and simmering. Each type of dish is supplied with a set of instructions which should be followed when using.

Browning grill
Some microwave ovens incorporate a radiant electric grill which is usually sited in the roof of the cooking cavity. This can be used to crisp or brown foods after cooking or, in some of the more advanced models, during cooking.

Combination oven
As the name suggests, combination ovens incorporate microwave power with conventional cooking facilities. Depending upon the model, these can be operated either separately, in sequence or at the same time, combining the speed of microwave energy with the browning and crisping qualities of conventional cooking by heat.

Conduction
The way heat spreads from one layer to the next. This is an important part of the microwave cooking process and is how foods continue to cook after being removed from the microwave. It is also the reason why microwave-proof plates get hot in the microwave oven — it's not the plate that is being heated up by the microwaves but the food it contains, and the heat generated by the hot food heats up the plate.

Defrosting
The process by which ice crystals revert to moisture as food thaws. As the pattern of ice crystals in foods is not uniform, thawing is often uneven. For even thawing, set the microwave on Defrost. This pulses out energy at regular intervals so the temperature of the food evens out between bursts.

Density
The density of different foods affects the length of time they need to cook, defrost and reheat. The denser the food, the longer the cooking time it will require. The density of containers also affects cooking times in the same way.

Door seals
Although microwave ovens vary in design, all have door seals which run around the perimeter of the door's interior. The seal consists of a metal channel filled with absorbent material to reduce the risk of any microwaves escaping while the oven is in use.

Hot spots
Although modern microwave ovens incorporate at least one device to help distribute the microwave energy evenly throughout the cooking cavity, hot spots may still exist. Find out where your oven's hot spots are by following the test on p. 124. The existence of hot spots necessitates food being turned, stirred and rearranged for even results.

Magnetron
A high-frequency radar tube that converts electrical energy into microwave energy.

Microwave thermometer
A thermometer specially designed for use in the microwave. Traditional thermometers cannot be used because the mercury is affected by microwaves.

Piercing
Any item covered by a membrane or skin must be pierced before being microwaved. This is to allow steam to escape during cooking and to prevent anything bursting from the pressure. Any boiling bags used in the oven should first be pierced to prevent too much steam building up inside.

Rearranging
Some items need rearranging in the microwave oven in order to cook evenly (see p. 128).

Shielding
A technique used to protect delicate areas of food from receiving too much microwave energy during cooking, by covering them with smooth strips of foil. Always follow your oven's manufacturer's guidelines when employing this technique and only use the minimum amount of foil.

Splash guard
Some wave stirrers are protected from food spatterings by a splash guard. This should be cleaned regularly according to the manufacturer's instructions.

Stacking
Plates of food being reheated should be stacked one above the other using microproof stacking rings or upturned plates as separators (see p. 129).

Standing time
This is an essential part of microwave cookery and allows food to continue cooking by conduction after the microwave energy has been turned off.

Stirring
A most important technique used in microwave cookery to distribute heat and help foods, particularly liquids, cook evenly. Always stir from the edges to the centre (see p. 127).

Tenting
This is the method of covering foods with foil once they have been removed from the oven so that they keep their heat during their standing time.

Variable power
A setting control that offers a range of energy outputs. The different powers available may be expressed in numerals, words, or percentages (see p. 118). The lower powers are usually achieved by pulsing the microwave energy on and off for varying lengths of time.

Wave guide
A metal duct that directs microwave energy produced by the magnetron into the oven cavity.

Wave stirrer
A device sited close to the wave guide outlet, designed to distribute the emerging microwaves evenly throughout the cooking cavity.

INDEX

140

Acknowledgments

Author's acknowledgments

I would like to thank Roselyne Masselin, Jo Wright and Beverley Muir for all their help in testing recipes; David Sulkin and Michael Hunter for eating most of the results, and Harriet Cruickshank for her support and enthusiasm. My thanks also to Liz Storer for typing the manuscript, Linda Fraser for testing selected recipes at 500W, and Felicity Jackson for editing the recipes and giving me so many good tips. As usual, the team at Dorling Kindersley have been wonderful, particularly Anita Ruddell on co-ordinating the design work and Carolyn Ryden for overseeing the whole book and patiently keeping me to deadlines.

Dorling Kindersley would like to thank: Felicity Jackson for her work on the recipes and Making the Most of Your Microwave Oven; Linda Fraser for testing recipes and giving practical advice; Hilary Bird for the index; Karl Adamson, assistant to Clive Streeter; Sanyo and Toshiba for the loan of microwave machines for photography and testing recipes in; Corning Microwave Cookware for the loan of equipment; the Electricity Council and the Microwave Association for providing helpful information.

Photography: Clive Streeter

Stylist: Alison Meldrum

Food preparation: Lyn Rutherford

Illustrators: Jane Cradock-Watson
pp. 6, 30, 37, 43, 69, 84, 92, 102, 113, 119, 120-9, 134-6
Brian Sayers
pp. 114-5, 116-7, 118

Typesetting: Modern Text Typesetting

Reproduction: Colourscan, Singapore